Lisa Moessing

Lobbying Uncovered?

Lobbying Registration in the European Union and the United States

**AN INTERDISCIPLINARY SERIES
OF THE CENTRE FOR INTERCULTURAL AND EUROPEAN STUDIES**

**INTERDISZIPLINÄRE SCHRIFTENREIHE
DES CENTRUMS FÜR INTERKULTURELLE UND EUROPÄISCHE STUDIEN**

CINTEUS · Fulda University of Applied Sciences · Hochschule Fulda

ISSN 1865-2255

8   *Janina Henning*
    In Dubio Pro Europa?
    An Analysis of the European External Action Structures
    after the Treaty of Lisbon
    ISBN 978-3-8382-0298-1

9   *Claas Oehlmann*
    Europa auf dem Weg zur Recycling-Gesellschaft?
    Die EU-Rohstoffinitiative im Kontext der Strategie Europa 2020
    ISBN 978-3-8382-0401-7

10 *Volker Hinnenkamp / Hans-Wolfgang Platzer (Eds. / Hrsg.)*
    Interkulturalität und Europäische Integration
    ISBN 978-3-8382-0573-1

11 *Vera Axyonova*
    The European Union's Democratization Policy for Central Asia
    Failed in Success or Succeeded in Failure?
    ISBN 978-3-8382-0614-1

12 *Lisa Moessing*
    Lobbying Uncovered?
    Lobbying Registration in the European Union and the United States
    ISBN 978-3-8382-0616-5

Series Editors

Gudrun Hentges
Volker Hinnenkamp
Anne Honer †
Hans-Wolfgang Platzer

Fachbereich Sozial- und Kulturwissenschaften
Hochschule Fulda University of Applied Sciences
Marquardstraße 35
D-36039 Fulda
cinteus@sk.hs-fulda.de
www.cinteus.eu

Lisa Moessing

LOBBYING UNCOVERED?

Lobbying Registration in the
European Union and the United States

ibidem-Verlag
Stuttgart

Bibliografische Information der Deutschen Nationalbibliothek
Die Deutsche Nationalbibliothek verzeichnet diese Publikation in der
Deutschen Nationalbibliografie; detaillierte bibliografische Daten sind im
Internet über http://dnb.d-nb.de abrufbar.

Bibliographic information published by the Deutsche Nationalbibliothek
Die Deutsche Nationalbibliothek lists this publication in the Deutsche Nationalbibliografie;
detailed bibliographic data are available in the Internet at http://dnb.d-nb.de.

∞

Gedruckt auf alterungsbeständigem, säurefreien Papier
Printed on acid-free paper

ISSN: 1865-2255

ISBN-13: 978-3-8382-0616-5

© *ibidem*-Verlag
Stuttgart 2014

Alle Rechte vorbehalten

Das Werk einschließlich aller seiner Teile ist urheberrechtlich geschützt. Jede Verwertung
außerhalb der engen Grenzen des Urheberrechtsgesetzes ist ohne Zustimmung des Verlages
unzulässig und strafbar. Dies gilt insbesondere für Vervielfältigungen,
Übersetzungen, Mikroverfilmungen und elektronische Speicherformen sowie die
Einspeicherung und Verarbeitung in elektronischen Systemen.

All rights reserved. No part of this publication may be reproduced, stored in or introduced into a retrieval
system, or transmitted, in any form, or by any means (electronical, mechanical, photocopying, recording or
otherwise) without the prior written permission of the publisher. Any person who does any unauthorized act
in relation to this publication may be liable to criminal prosecution and civil claims for damages.

Printed in Germany

Editorial

This series is intended as a publication panel of the Centre of Intercultural and European Studies (CINTEUS) at Fulda University of Applied Sciences. The series aims at making research results, anthologies, conference readers, study books and selected qualification theses accessible to the general public. It comprises of scientific and interdisciplinary works on inter- and transculturality; the European Union from an interior and a global perspective; and problems of social welfare and social law in Europe. Each of these are fields of research and teaching in the Social- and Cultural Studies Faculty at Fulda University of Applied Sciences and its Centre for Intercultural and European Studies. We also invite contributions from outside the faculty that share and enrich our research.

Gudrun Hentges, Volker Hinnenkamp, Anne Honer & Hans-Wolfgang Platzer

Editorial

Die Buchreihe versteht sich als Publikationsforum des Centrums für interkulturelle und europäische Studien (CINTEUS) der Hochschule Fulda. Ziel der CINTEUS-Reihe ist es, Forschungsergebnisse, Anthologien, Kongressreader, Studienbücher und ausgewählte Qualifikationsarbeiten einer interessierten Öffentlichkeit zugänglich zu machen. Die Reihe umfasst fachwissenschaftliche und interdisziplinäre Arbeiten aus den Bereichen Inter- und Transkulturalität, Europäische Union aus Binnen- und globaler Perspektive sowie wohlfahrtsstaatliche und sozialrechtliche Probleme Europas. All dies sind Fachgebiete, die im Fachbereich Sozial- und Kulturwissenschaften der Hochschule Fulda University of Applied Sciences und dem angegliederten Centrum für interkulturelle und Europastudien gelehrt und erforscht werden. Ausdrücklich eingeladen an der Publikationsreihe mitzuwirken sind auch solche Studien, die nicht 'im Hause' entstanden sind, aber CINTEUS-Schwerpunkte berühren und bereichern.

Gudrun Hentges, Volker Hinnenkamp, Anne Honer & Hans-Wolfgang Platzer

Foreword

Ever since its early days, the process of European Integration has been accompanied by interest intermediation of societal actors. During the past decades, the scene of EU lobby organizations has been continuously growing. This development and the important role lobbyism plays in EU decision making processes have caused heavy interest among academic researchers. Today EU lobbyism can be seen as one of the most important research fields within EU Studies.

The study at hand is a valuable and innovative contribution to the scientific research in EU lobbyism for several reasons.

Its overall research perspective is to explore the EU's efforts in making lobbyism more transparent. After years of discussions and contested negotiations, the EU established a voluntary Transparency Register in 2011.

This book is one of the first systematic comparisons of the voluntary Transparency Register of the European Union with the mandatory Transparency Register of the United States. An essential part of the study is shaped by the perceptions of personnel of European institutions, Brussels-based lobbyists, and lobby critics. These qualitative empirical findings, gained by semi-structured interviews, allow for deep insights into the practical working mechanisms of the EU's Transparency Register, its applicability and efficiency, its problems and shortcomings.

Dealing with the topic of "democratic EU governance—transparency—EU lobbyism," this book addresses a broad audience of politically interested readers.

Hans-Wolfgang Platzer

Fulda, June 2014

Contents

Index of abbreviations, figures, and tables 11

Preamble 15

1 Introduction 17
1.1 Problem statement 17
1.2 Research objectives 18
1.3 State of research 19
1.4 Research question 20
1.5 Method 21
1.5.1 Choice of method and implementation 21
1.5.2 Restrictions of research design 28
1.5.3 Evaluation 28
1.6 Structure of the book 29

2 Conceptual background 31
2.1 Political systems of the EU and the United States 31
2.1.1 Political system of the EU 31
2.1.2 Decision-making in the EU 34
2.1.3 Political system of the United States 39
2.1.4 Decision-making in the United States 41
2.2 Influencing political decision-making 44
2.2.1 Lobbying 44
2.2.2 Interest groups 48
2.2.3 History of lobbying regulation in the EU 49
2.2.4 Lobbying in the EU 55
2.2.5 History of lobbying regulation in the United States 59
2.2.6 Lobbying in the United States 63
2.2.7 Interim conclusion 66
2.3 Regulation and registration 68
2.4 Transparency 69

3 Comparison of lobbying registration in the EU and the United States ... 71

3.1 The European Union ... 71
3.1.1 Implementation of the Transparency Register ... 71
3.1.2 Legal basis ... 75
3.1.3 Instruments of control and penalties ... 79
3.1.4 Effectiveness and criticism ... 82

3.2 The United States of America ... 86
3.2.1 Implementation of the Lobbying Disclosure Act ... 86
3.2.2 Legal basis ... 93
3.2.3 Instruments of control and penalties ... 94
3.2.4 Effectiveness and criticism ... 97

4 Result subsumption, discussion, and perspectives ... 101
4.1 Conclusion on the comparison ... 101
4.2 Discussion ... 112
4.3 Incentives for improvement ... 131
4.4 Incentives for further research ... 135

5 References ... 137

6 Annex ... 147
6.1 Databases ... 147
6.2 Interview manual ... 149
6.3 Interviewee overview ... 150

Index of abbreviations, figures, and tables

ABBREVIATIONS

ALTER-EU	Alliance for Lobbying Transparency and Ethics Regulation
BDI	*Bundesverband der Deutschen Industrie e.V.* (The Voice of German Industry)
BM	Burson-Marsteller
CHR	Clerk of the House of Representatives
COREPER	Committee of Permanent Representatives
CRP	Center for Responsive Politics
DG	Directorate-General
DLR	*Deutsches Zentrum für Luft- und Raumfahrt* (German Aerospace Center)
ECJ	European Court of Justice
ECSC	European Coal and Steel Community
EP	European Parliament
ETI	European Transparency Initiative
EU	European Union
FARA	Foreign Agents Registration Act
FRLA	Federal Regulation of Lobbying Act
GAO	US Government Accountability Office
GSC	General Secretariat of the Council
HLOGA	Honest Leadership and Open Government Act
IIA	Interinstitutional Agreement
JTRS	Joint Transparency Register Secretariat
LDA	Lobbying Disclosure Act
LD-1	Lobbying registration (United States)
LD-2	Activity-related and financial reports (United States)
LD-203	Certain contributions reports (United States)
MEP	Member of European Parliament
MP	Member of Parliament
OECD	Organisation for Economic Co-operation and Development
OLP	Ordinary Legislative Procedure
PAC	Political Action Committee
ROIR	Register of Interest Representatives

SOS	Secretary of the Senate
TEU	Treaty on EU
TFEU	Treaty on the Functioning of the EU
TR	Transparency Register
WWF	World Wide Fund for Nature

FIGURES

Figure 1. Transparency register—weekly evolution of registrants 83
Figure 2. Number of US lobbyists 98

TABLES

Table 1. Classification of tendency indicators 23
Table 2. Interviewee overview 27
Table 3. JTRS checks on TR registrants 80
Table 4. Comparison overview 101
Table 5. Discussion overview 125

Preamble

The motivation for bringing about this book originated from the general question whether lobbying proves to be as opaque, influential, and malicious as the image of the profession seems to be publicly maintained, and which measures of control can be imposed. Considering that the mandatory registration system installed in the United States is obviously perceived as a role model for the disclosure of lobbying, it has been a key incentive for the author to examine it in detail, which further allows identifying possible weaknesses of this model register as well. Moreover, by recommending measures of improvement, the author actively participates in the discussion about the revision of the European Union's Transparency Register. Special thanks are dedicated to all interviewees, who have contributed to this book through personal, e-mail, or phone interviews or simply by providing additional information. Particularly with regard to personal expertise with registration mechanisms, the scope of research of this book and its constructive analysis would not have been possible without the inputs from key respondents. The reason for some interviewees to be quoted in anonymity is not only based on the fact that lobbyism is still a sensitive issue, but also that, in some cases, views are personal and cannot be authorized as an official view of the entity represented by the individual. Therefore, especially the statements made by the interviewed Council Official cannot be regarded as an official opinion.[1]

---

[1] The term 'American' in this book alludes to the United States of America, whereas 'European' refers to the European Union. 'The Council' is short for 'The Council of the European Union'.

1 Introduction

1.1 Problem statement

Today lobbying tends to be approached as a rather mysterious and nontransparent profession, which seeks to tailor legislation to its ends and is seen to occur as a gray area of politics.[2] Several regulative mechanisms have been implemented in the past to monitor such activities in various democratic countries in an effort to increase the transparency of lobbying and to enhance an open dialogue between political leadership, interest representatives, and the public. One of the most recent mechanisms is the Transparency Register (TR) of the European Union (EU), which was launched in 2011 jointly by the European Parliament (EP) and the European Commission as part of the European Transparency Initiative (ETI). Despite the ambitious approach and an increasing amount of registrants, regulation remains voluntary. The register lacks a clear and detailed definition of 'the lobbyist' as such, disclosure requirements are partially misleading, and sufficient incentives for registration are still intensively debated. In contrast, the mandatory register in the United States is often referred to as one of the most advanced concepts of lobbying disclosure and frequently serves as an argument used by critics of the EU's voluntary approach. The US register was a result of the Lobbying Disclosure Act (LDA) in 1995; however, it is still imperfect in its conception. The study at hand contrasts both approaches by their scope and legal basis, identifies current weaknesses and strengths, and points out criticism. Based on these findings and by the involvement of personal expertise of lobbyists, EU and US officials, scholars and lobby critics, this thesis identifies areas of the European model that require improvement. The book is also designed to enlighten its readers that even if the profession of lobbyists still maintains a huge influential power on political decision-making, it is not necessarily as opaque and negative as usually conveyed, if one only takes a closer look.

The findings of this book can be a complementary input to the revision process of the TR for various reasons: First, since the European register has been launched in 2011, it is still relatively new and without a doubt has still not been examined to a satisfactory extent. Second, a policy process created and shaped by 28 Member States obviously requires critical input from its citizens.

---

[2] Leif, T. and Speth, R. (eds.), (¹2003). Die stille Macht. Lobbyismus in Deutschland. Wiesbaden: Westdeutscher Verlag, p. 8.

Third, specific measures, regulations, and instruments of a certain political system should permanently be contrasted with other existing concepts, which is realized by this book through its analysis of a North American register. Finally, as research will disclose, resources of the Joint Transparency Register Secretariat (JTRS) are limited. Thus, the possibility for the conduction of broader research related to the register is assumed to be restricted as well.

1.2 Research objectives

The study at hand is not designed to merely provide a comparison between two different registration systems, it also aims at extending its scope beyond. Its unique approach lies in its **combination of a detailed comparison between a voluntary TR (EU) and a mandatory register (United States)**, complemented by a **critical discussion on the European registration method in particular**. Therefore, this work is one of the first to contrast the US registration system with the TR as the most recent and advanced disclosure mechanism in the EU. An essential part of the discussion is designed to critically and constructively formulate amending options for the European system, through input and experience from personnel of European institutions, Brussels-based lobbyists, and lobby critics. Beyond that, this book will also formulate incentives for future research and identify future perspectives. Due to its focus on the EU, this thesis goes beyond previous research in that it discusses the extension of access passes to the Commission and the possibility of including the Council of the EU as the third official EU operator of the register. The first published official study about the legal basis of a mandatory register in the EU will also be considered. Further scientific intention of this book is to convey a preliminary general understanding about the concept of lobbying and related activities with respect to the differing political preconditions in the democratic systems of the EU and the United States.

This book will provide an overview of the particular historic developments of lobbying regulation, differentiate between specific characteristics of both the registers, and describe strengths and weaknesses inherent to both approaches. With regard to their legal basis, it points out the legal prerequisites, which both approaches require, and allows to gain insight into the daily applicability of the EU register. Accordingly, it deduces from that where the European concept still leaves room for amendments. This study is addressed to scholars, academics, interest representatives, and members of the public with a general interest in lobbying regulation or a concern on regulative mechanisms in the

EU and the United States in particular. Especially in terms of the current revision procedure of the European TR, this thesis is directed toward individuals of EU institutions and designed to serve as an inspiring input to the debate.

1.3 State of research

This chapter will give a brief overview of important theories and key literature related to this book. Existing examinations and theories about concepts of lobbying and lobbying registration range from a variety of approaches: They include Rinus van Schendelen's perception of a unique 'Brussels method' of interest insourcing; the assumption of Hix, Høyland, and Buholzer that interest procurement in the EU has to respect a specific multilevel order; Sebaldt's concept of dominating issue networks in the United States; and the theory of Kraft that lobbyists overseas have nearly gained a shared decision-making competence. Especially with regard to the applicability of the US register to the TR and a comparison of both in particular, scientific theories remain rather rare. While some scholars have contrasted lobbying regulation in the EU with the United States,[3] comparisons often remain on a rather general and superficial level and do not examine both the registration systems in detail. The current state of information shows that little literature has focused on the TR. Few authors have dedicated research to the EU's latest register; the latter is rather addressed in scientific reports and short essays, if at all. Especially in terms of the legal basis of this register, the first official scientific study was launched in June 2013. Thus, scientific expertise here has limited validity.

A key report among the literature analyzed for this book is the Annual Report of 2012 of the JTRS, since the latter is not only the TR's official operator but furthermore a key institution in the context of this work. Furthermore, critical reports such as "Dodgy Data. Time to fix the EU's Transparency Register" (2012) and "Rescue the Register! How to make EU lobby transparency credible and reliable" (2013) are considered. Both have been published by a representative Brussels-based lobby critical organization, namely the Alliance for Lobbying Transparency and Ethics Regulation (ALTER-EU). The JTRS report mainly concentrates on the effect of the register after its first year of running in a self-reflective and self-critical way, and gives an overview on aspects to be possibly included into the register's review process. In contrast, both reports of

---

[3] See e.g., Holman (2009), Holman and Luneburg (2012), or Kraft (2006).

ALTER-EU mainly focus on the deficits of the register. Both reports are rather one sided.[4] However, the thesis at hand will consider both views equally.

Key literature providing a foundation for this study are the book by Eising and Kohler-Koch (2005), defining approaches and tactics of interest representatives based on the European multilevel system of governance, as well as the findings of Eising and Lehringer (2010) with a more distinct focus on interest groups. The latter are complemented by a wide-ranging analysis of EU lobbying, published by Michalowitz in 2007. Also Coen and Richardson (2011) elicit the new volume of interest representation and newly developed tactics in the EU, whereas Hix and Høyland (2011) provide a comprehensive overview of the system of the EU. Due to its focus on the EU's latest register version, a recent study of Gentili (2013) is one of the most current resources and an inspiring work on which this research is developed. Likewise, the research by Kraft (2006), who compares previous lobbying regulation in the EU to similar structures in the United States, is an essential input. The work of Berry (1997) provides a detailed overview of interest groups on the other side of the Atlantic, which is complemented by the publication of Rosenthal (1993), who broadly defines characteristics of US lobbyists and their profession. Finally, Holman (2008, 2009) and Holman and Luneburg (2012) critically approach both concepts of disclosure and previous reforms.

1.4 Research question

The scientific aim of this book is to contrast the registration system of the EU with that of the United States, and to measure its effectiveness and efficiency. In the context of this book and as defined by the author, **effectiveness** refers to possible effects caused by register-linked perception, legislation, accessibility, handling, or technical conditions that can lead to certain consequences. However, the latter do not necessarily have to be related to efficiency. **Efficiency** alludes to register-linked perception, legislation, accessibility, handling, or technical conditions that may evoke more efficient conditions than before, such as by saving time or work.

---

[4] Gentili, A. (2013). Transparency Register, Work in Progress. Evaluation of the Register's Effectiveness Before Its Second Anniversary and Its Review. Evaluation Report. http://www.europeanpublicaffairs.eu/wp-content/uploads/2013/06/Transparency-Register_Evaluation-report_Andrea-Gentili.pdf, visited on June 11, 2013, p. 1.

Hereby, the general research question is as follows:

➲ **How effective and efficient is the EU's TR in comparison to lobbying registration in the United States, and to what extent can both the effectiveness and efficiency of the EU register be increased?**

For a complementary analysis, the objects of research shall be examined pursuant to the following underlying subquestions:

➲ **In which facets do both registers differ and resemble each other?**

➲ **Can the US approach be taken as a reference model for the EU register?**

➲ **How do relevant actors and addressees of influence assess the EU register?**

➲ **Accordingly, should the EU register become mandatory?**

➲ **As regards the EU register, where can incentives for improvement be identified?**

1.5 Method

The following chapter is designed to explain the methods applied for the research of this study. According to the particular research questions, the methodical approaches will each be presented in brief. Complementarily, a list of indicators will be defined with regard to 'measuring' the research aspects at hand. Further content of this chapter is formed by a detailed enumeration of interviewees and a display of restrictions of research design.

1.5.1 Choice of method and implementation

The study relies on an **empirical-analytical** approach and employs the following methods to answer the respective research questions:

➲ **In which facets do both registers differ and resemble each other?**

Answers will be generated by a detailed comparison, which to a major extent will be based on document analysis and the examination of both registers online, as well as some background information generated by interviews. To simplify the complexity of extensive comparisons, systems will be examined in succession, starting with the EU. To summarize the results, the two tables are designed for giving a better overview of differences and similarities of both registers.

- Can the US approach be taken as a reference model for the EU register?
- How do relevant actors and addressees of influence assess the EU register?

Input for both questions will be acquired by actors' perception complemented by an analysis of literature, legal documents, and official studies and reports. Actors' perception is provided by lobbyists, political representatives from the EU and the United States, EU lobbying experts, and watch dog representatives. Answers will be generated by qualitative semistructured interviews based on a partly standardized interview manual. Equally important sources are speeches of EU officials and visual materials, such as the movie "The Brussels Business."[5]

- Accordingly, should the EU register become mandatory?

Even if a variety of literature and official reports have already discussed this question to a major degree, the experience, insights, and positions of EU key institutions as well as interest representatives is necessary to answer this question. In particular, the qualitative actors and expert interviews will form an essential basis for discussion.

- Accordingly, where can incentives for improvement be identified?

Inspiration for key starting points to improve the EU register will be mainly generated by actors' perception via qualitative interviews and e-mail requests. This method will be complemented by research of literature, legal documents, as well as official reports and studies, and by examination of particular registers online. Registers will be examined by content, accessibility, and legal basis.

- How effective and efficient is the EU's TR in comparison to lobbying registration in the United States, and to what extent can both the effectiveness and efficiency of the EU register be increased?

This question will be answered by the four subquestions and, thus, by the aforementioned methods. Where necessary, research will be complemented by further literature research, including the analysis of legal documents, scientific articles, reports, studies, and official governmental information accessible online.

---

[5] Produced by Steven Dhoedt and Friedrich Moser, released in 2012.

Table 1. Classification of tendency indicators

For measuring the questions-related aspects of research, the following tendency indicators[6] have been specified in table 1.:

Tendency indicator	Intention of measurement
➲ The current number of registrants compared with the starting amount	Increase in registrants, acceptance among interest representatives for the particular tool
➲ Results of the technical and content-related comparison between both registers	Differences and similarities, accessibility, starting points for improvement, efficiency, effectiveness
➲ Incentivizing of registration with the EU register	Acceptances among EU registrants and nonregistrants, efficiency, effectiveness
➲ The complexity of registration requirements of the EU register as identified by analysis of the qualitative expert and actors interviews	Perception of complexity, everyday handling, effectiveness, starting points for improvement
➲ The perception among lobbyists of current consequences for non-compliance with the TR's regulations	Effectiveness of consequences, starting points for improvement
➲ The perception of the monitoring system of the EU's register	Effectiveness and efficiency of monitoring system, starting points for improvement
➲ The overall attitude among interest representatives concerning the voluntary configuration of the EU register	Effectiveness of the voluntary configuration, classifying arguments for and against a mandatory register

By combining various methods and indicators, the book at hand is designed to direct a scope of questions to the object of research, which should be as broad

---

[6] "Tendency" because they simply indicate a certain tendency only, but cannot guarantee a matter of fact.

as possible. An additional value of this study is established by involving insider perspectives of European institutions' personnel as well as interest representatives. Therefore, it is based to a major degree on interviews of qualitative experts, especially that of actors. The latter are perceived as the favored approach compared to quantitative interviews due to the following reasons: First, qualitative interviews allow for individual, subjective answers that are an essential tool, especially with regards to detailed personal experiences with the registration process, personal perceptions of the EU policy process, and constructive approaches for improvement. By that, this method afterwards allows explaining, understanding, and interpreting certain correlations simply; also classifications can be more easily generated. Second, such detailed information as gained through qualitative interviews cannot be provided by any scientific literature. As a third reason, qualitative semistructured interviews can be 'tailored' individually to the interviewee by a partly standardized interview manual and simply allow for further enquiries to clarify statements or additional questions that might arise. Nonetheless, the questions designed for the Brussels-based interest representatives are to a certain degree standardized for reasons of comparability, but have always been 'tailored' to the individual entity and person.

The interviews were all transcribed after they had been conducted. Further work included categorizing the answers that were referring to the same aspects and interpreting statements to develop theses. Particularly important here were the categorization and selection of answers referring to the discussion about the TR, its sanctions and potentials for improvement, as well as their summary for a discussion overview. Another important part of the interview analysis was to develop new questions for the interview manual in case they originate as a consequence of interviewees' answers. Interviews have mainly been conducted in person; in case it is impossible, phone calls or e-mail enquiries have been used. All the interviews ranged 30-40 minutes in length. Research and interviews have been accomplished during the TR's second year of operation, with the revision of the register starting in June 2013.

More precisely, the following representatives of the three EU key bodies as well as of the EU register's key institution have been interviewed: A collaborator of the JTRS, referred to as **'JTRS Staff'**; a Member and Vice President of the European Parliament who will be referred to as **'MEP'**; a Member of the Cabinet of Commission Vice President Maroš Šefčovič, Commissioner for Inter-Institutional Relations and Administration, referred to as the **'Commission Representative'**; an Official working for the General Secretariat of the Council

(GSC) of the EU, who will be entitled the **'GSC Representative'**; and another Official of the Council's Secretariat, who, due to more broader responses, will be referred to as the **'Council Official.'** Further input could be gained through an e-mail interview with one of the distinguished present-day scholars on EU lobbying, who will be mentioned as **'EU Lobbying Expert.'**

The interviewee selection covers both national and European associations, as well as four of the following categories of the EU register (emphasized in boldface): **Professional consultancies/law firms/self-employed consultants; In-house lobbyists and trade/professional associations; Nongovernmental organizations (NGOs); Think tanks, research and academic institutions;** Organizations representing churches and religious communities; and Organizations representing local, regional, and municipal authorities, other public or mixed entities.

Respondents on the part of interest representatives are the following:

- An employee of the Brussels office of the PR and communications firm *Burson-Marsteller* (BM), representing professional consultancies, and referred to as **'the BM Consultant.'**

- The Head of Brussels office of one of the 10 biggest European companies who accordingly will be cited as the **'In-House Lobbyist.'**

- A member of the Brussels European Policy Office of the World Wide Fund for Nature (WWF), representing NGOs and entitled **'the WWF Employee.'**

- An associate of the Brussels office of the *German Aerospace Center* (*Deutsches Zentrum für Luft- und Raumfahrt*, DLR) as a think tank representative, named **'the DLR Employee.'**

- A member of the Brussels representation of *The German Business Representation* (*Bundesverband der Deutschen Industrie e.V.*, BDI), covering national associations, being referred to as **'the BDI Employee.'**

- An associate of *BUSINESSEUROPE*, the "main horizontal business organisation at EU level"[7] and thus a European association, named **'the BUSINESSEUROPE Employee.'**

- A representative of euRobotics, a newly established European association, entitled as **'the euRobotics Employee.'**

---

[7] BUSINESSEUROPE. (2013). Mission and Priorities. http://www.businesseurope.eu/content/default.asp?PageID=582, visited on July 6, 2013.

Representatives of churches or religious communities have not been interviewed as this category accounts for just 0.56 percent of the total registrants.[8] For closing the gap between the EU as the TR's operator and lobbyists as its registrants, this study furthermore includes the view of a former employee of the Brussels-based *ALTER-EU*, cited as **'the EU Watchdog Representative.'** By that, this work also involves the standpoint of a watchdog organization that monitors the EU register's development and is perceived "as the most vocal watchdog in the transparency arena of Brussels" by the JTRS Staff.[9] This organization has been selected, since—according to its own information—its coalition is formed by more than 200 entities,[10] such as regional and head offices of Corporate Europe Observatory, Friends of the Earth, LobbyControl, Greenpeace, Transparency International, etc. For gaining more details on the lobbying disclosure system of the United States, the following US interviewees provided insight through e-mail: A Government Affairs Lobbyist working for *Public Citizen's Congress Watch* and referred to as **'the US Watchdog Representative,'** as well as a Senior Researcher at the *Center for Responsive Politics* (CRP), cited as **'the CRP Representative.'** A telephone interview has been conducted with an employee of the Clerk of the House, House of Representatives, who will be referred to as **'the CHR Employee.' A general overview of all interviewees will be provided by table 2.**

---

[8] As of July 2013.
[9] JTRS Staff. (2013c). E-mail received on May 27, 2013.
[10] ALTER-EU. (n.d.) About ALTER-EU. http://www.alter-eu.org/about, visited on July 10, 2013.

Table 2. Interviewee overview

Actors'/experts' names	Institutions
BDI Employee, member of the Brussels office of The German Business Representation (BDI), Actor	The German Business Representation, national association
BM Consultant, employee of the Brussels office of the PR and communications firm Burson-Marsteller, Actor	Burson-Marsteller, professional consultancy
BUSINESSEUROPE Employee, associate of BUSINESSEUROPE, Actor	BUSINESS EUROPE, horizontal European business association
CHR Employee, representing the Clerk of the House, House of Representatives, Actor	House of Representatives, US Congress
Commission Representative, Member of the Cabinet of Commission Vice President Maroš Šefčovič, Commissioner for Inter-Institutional Relations and Administration, Actor	EU Commission
CRP Representative, Senior Researcher at the CRP, Expert	CRP, Watchdog Organization
Council Official, Official of the Council's Secretariat, Actor	Council of the EU
DLR Employee, member of the Brussels office of the *German Aerospace Center* (DLR), Actor	German Aerospace Center, Think tanks, research and academic institutions
EU Lobbying Expert, one of the most important recent scholars on EU lobbying, Expert	European University, Scientist
euRobotics Employee, representative of euRobotics, a newly established European association, Actor	euRobotics, European association
EU Watchdog Representative, former employee of the Brussels-based ALTER-EU, Actor	ALTER-EU, Watchdog organization
GSC Representative, Official working for the GSC of the EU, Actor	Council of the EU
In-House Lobbyist, Head of Brussels office of one of the 10 biggest European companies, Actor	Industrial representative, In-house lobbyists and trade/professional associations
JTRS Staff, Actor	JTRS
MEP, Member and Vice President of the EP, Actor	EP
US Watchdog Representative, Government Affairs Lobbyist working for Public Citizen's Congress Watch, Expert	Public Citizen's Congress Watch, Watchdog organization
WWF Employee, member of the Brussels European Policy Office of the WWF, Actor	WWF, NGOs

1.5.2 Restrictions of research design

Since the qualitative interviews that were conducted with representatives from the United States had outrun the frame of this thesis, the research on registrants' experience and a general perception of the registration system as such is limited to Brussels-based lobbyists. Furthermore, this book neither includes an analysis related to the effectiveness of the register-linked code of conduct, nor the respective codes of conduct for deputies. Actors' perception remains limited to qualitative interviews and an overview of opinions and tendencies instead of value-based charts, since a quantitative survey among Brussels-based lobbyists is assumed to have possibly acquired fewer results than an individual addressing of interviewees. Apart from that, it would have required a far greater sample of respondents to guarantee scientific representativeness. To keep its scope balanced, the author has identified the EP, the European Commission, the Council of the EU, as well as the US Congress as key bodies for lobbying in this book, since they form the main addressees for legislative influence. Therefore, the analysis of this book is limited to these institutions.

Generally, the study at hand is not based on *one* single scientific theory of lobbying, since the complexity of this field simply requires a broader approach (see Chapter 2.2.1). However, it takes into account various scientific and theoretical approaches of interest representation. Furthermore, it is not the aim of this book to contrast both lobbying registers against a certain theoretical approach, but to compare their concepts and identify incentives for improvement especially for the European lobby register.

1.5.3 Evaluation

Despite the fact that this book considers a variety of US and especially EU actors and their particular perceptions of the registers, for a more scientifically reliable validity it would have been more ideal to gather and evaluate perceptions of more US actors. Even if findings cannot be generalized due to a lack of a scientifically representative amount of respondents, the actors' and experts' perceptions allow for enough insight to identify certain tendencies regarding scientific concerns about daily work and handling of both registers. Due to technical problems in downloading LDA databases for a complementary research of this book, accessibility of registrant data was limited and thus decreases the validity of the comparison of both registers. Another lack of comparability consists of inconsistent numbers of registrants provided by the Secretary of the Senate (SOS) and the Clerk of the House of Representatives (CHR). Generally, information about registration and lobbying regulation could be gained more easily through EU sources: Official requests to the US government were sometimes simply not answered, automatically generated, or too general to be helpful. With regard to personal inquiry, further key questions were developed during the interview phase. As a consequence, not all actors could comment on those questions, even if the underlying method was the conduction of qualitative interviews. Generally, the author assesses a debate about the TR limited in its significance as long as data about its actual target group, especially MEPs and their staff, are either not accessible or not existent. However, this book provides a helpful summary about main differences and similarities of both registers: It includes a basic overview of the effectiveness and efficiency of the TR, and defines a set of realistic additional ideas for improvement of lobbying registration.

1.6 Structure of the book

As a thematic instruction, this book presents a basic overview of the different political systems and decision-making procedures, defines the profession of lobbying with regard to particularities in the EU as well as the United States, and explains transparency from a political and scientific perspective, in Chapter 2. The comparative part of this book is formed by the sequential analysis of the particular systems, commencing with the EU. The analyses are followed by a table summarizing the most striking similarities and differences. Chapter 3 concludes by outlining comparison between key differences and affinities. Insights gained through interviews are mainly reflected in the discussion of Chapter 4, in which arguable aspects such as simplified filing requirements, incentives for registration, extension of the register's scope, and the register's voluntary constitution are addressed at length. Finally, in Chapter 5, this thesis offers starting points for improving the EU register and points out incentives for future research.

2 Conceptual background

This chapter will provide the conceptual background and a brief outline of the particular political systems and decision-making procedures as well as the historical background of lobbying regulation in the EU and the United States Further, it will define the concept of lobbying and point out differences in its practice with respect to both political systems. To conclude, this chapter will clarify the terms 'regulation' and 'registration,' 'interest groups,' and the concepts of 'transparency' and 'lobbying.'

2.1 Political systems of the EU and the United States

2.1.1 Political system of the EU

Whereas especially the integrative process of the EU is often described as intergovernmental,[11] the EU can also be defined as a **multilevel network** incorporating different degrees of supranational and trans-governmental interweaving of politics.[12] The political system of the Union is to a high degree decentralized,[13] as it is composed of a variety of legislative authorities at different levels; competences and areas of applicability partly overlap.[14] In addition, Eising and Lehringer explain the EU as a system that is "highly dynamic, horizontally and vertically differentiated and complex" and whose legislators favor consensus building.[15] Due to this special horizontal and vertical complexity, interest groups could choose from multiple access points to address the EU policy process.[16] The political constitution of the EU is furthermore characterized by an "imperfect dual legitimacy" since citizen interests are represented by the EP, whereas

---

[11] Eising, R. and Lehringer, S. (^{3}2010). Interest Groups and the European Union. In: M. Cini and N. Pérez-Solórzano Borragán (eds.), *European Union Politics*. New York: Oxford University Press, p. 446; see also M. Cini. (^{3}2010). Intergovernmentalism. In: M. Cini and N. Pérez-Solórzano Borragán (eds.), *European Union Politics*. New York: Oxford University Press, p. 87.
[12] See also Eising, R. and Kohler-Koch, B. (^{1}2005). Interessenpolitik im europäischen Mehrebenensystem. In: Eising, R. and Kohler-Koch, B. (eds.). *Interessenpolitik in Europa. Regieren in Europa 7*. Baden-Baden: Nomos, p. 11.
[13] Hix, S. and Høyland, B. (^{3}2011). *The Political System of the European Union. The European Union Series*. Houndmills/New York: Palgrave Macmillan, p. 15.
[14] Buholzer, R.P. (1998). *Legislatives Lobbying in der Europäischen Union. Ein Konzept für Interessengruppen*. Dissertation Nr. 2153; Universität Sankt Gallen. Bern: Verlag Paul Haupt, p. 154.
[15] Eising and Lehringer (^{3}2010), p. 190.
[16] Ibid., p. 193.

the Council of the EU represents the particular concerns of the Member States.[17] Simon Hix and Bjørn Høyland claimed that by delegating legislative, executive, and judicial powers, the EU acts rather unlike international organizations and more in the manner of a state. For instance, unlike Federal states, the Member States remain "the sovereign signatories of the EU Treaty" and maintain their sovereignty in some policy areas.[18]

The European Parliament

The EP incorporates seven political fractions. Its political mission is implemented by 20 standing committees, special temporary committees, and committees of inquiry.[19] Since its first ballot in 1979, the EP is not only the **EU's single directly elected political body**, but also the **only supranational parliament worldwide** representing more than 506.8 million citizens from 28 nations[20] by its current assembly of 766 Members after the accession of Croatia on July 1, 2013. However, this number will be reduced to 751 by 2014. Being considered as a **working parliament** that is re-elected every five years, MEPs are endowed with legislative, controlling, and budgetary power, as well as the power to approve and dismiss the Commission. The EP is empowered to adopt European law; its right of legislative initiative is pivotal here, as it can ask the Commission to draft a legislative proposal on a particular subject.[21] Furthermore, the EP's budgetary power as a co-decision maker covers all EU expenditure as well as common agricultural policy spending.[22] Due to several treaty changes, the EP has changed from a consultative body in 1951 to a co-legislator in the 21st century. Beyond that, the EP's plenary forms the world's second largest parliamentary assembly after the Chinese parliament.

The Council

The Council of the EU, also known as the Council of Ministers, represents the Union's 28 Member States and their political intentions. Its political agenda is served by technical working groups, attachés of the Member States' permanent

---

[17] Ibid., p. 194.
[18] Hix and Høyland (³2011), p. 12.
[19] European Parliament. (n.d.). Parliamentary Committees. http://www.europarl.europa.eu/aboutparliament/en/00aab6aedf/Committees.html, visited on July 13, 2013.
[20] Eurostat. (2013). Kroatien in der EU in Zahlen. Eurostat Press Release of June 25, 2013. http://epp.eurostat.ec.europa.eu/cache/ITY_PUBLIC/1-25062013-AP/DE/1-25062013-AP-DE.PDF, visited on July12, 2013.
[21] European Parliament. (2010). The European Parliament. Luxembourg: Publications Office of the European Union, p. 9.
[22] Ibid., p. 4.

representatives, the Committee of Permanent Representatives (COREPER), and Member States' ministers. The latter meet in 10 different Council configurations to make political decisions, which have been prepared by the former.[23] Despite covering nearly the whole bandwidth of national-level politics, the intensity of the Council of Ministers' involvement highly varies according to its competences laid down in the EU Treaties.[24] During recent years, the Council's mode of decision-making shifted away from unanimity to Qualified Majority Voting[25] and in special cases even to simple majority, and therefore from an intrastate mode to a supranational one, as the EU Lobbying Expert concludes.[26] Even if still remaining autonomous or the leading institution in rather sensitive aspects, such as taxes, the Common Foreign and Security Policy (CFSP), or economic policies respectively, the Council as a co-legislator has obviously become more dependent on the EP's decision within the legislative decision-making procedure.[27] However, the Council of Ministers is also endowed with the right of initiative to request a legislative proposal by the Commission and is characterized by the EU itself as the "Union's main decision-making body."[28]

The European Commission
Often referred to as the "guardian of the Treaties," the Union's executive body observes the correct application of Union law under the control of the European Court of Justice (ECJ). It represents the general interest of the EU, acts independently of the Member States' governments, and serves its duty "to propose and implement Community policies." Where Member States have transferred part of their legislative sovereignty to the Union, the Commission is endowed with a "quasi-exclusive right of initiative" of legislative proposals for those issues, which promote European integration, such as the internal market or Common Agricultural Policy. The Commission's right of legislative initiative is

---

[23] Consilium (n.d.). Council Configurations. http://www.consilium.europa.eu/council/council-configurations?lang=en, visited on July 13, 2013.
[24] Van Schendelen, R. (¹2012). Die Kunst des EU-Lobbyings. Erfolgreiches Public Affairs Management im Labyrinth Brüssels. Berlin: Lexxion Verlagsgesellschaft mbH Berlin, p. 61.
[25] Requires 65 percent of the EU's population as well as 55 percent of Member States from November 2014 onward.
[26] Van Schendelen (¹2012), p. 62f.
[27] Ibid., p. 63; see also: Europa. (n.d.d). Glossary: Council of the European Union. http://europa.eu/legislation_summaries/glossary/eu_council_en.htm, visited on July 15, 2013.
[28] Europa. (n.d.c) Glossary: Right of Initiative. http://europa.eu/legislation_summaries/glossary/initiative_right_en.htm, visited on July 13, 2013.

shared with the Members in areas of justice and internal affairs.[29] The scholar Daniel Naurin categorizes the Commission as the system's "main agenda-setter."[30] Pursuant to Nugent, the institution is involved in EU decision-making at all levels and fronts—hence, it is "at the very heart of the EU system."[31]

To serve its executive duties, the institution also executes the EU's budget and manages EU programs, for example.[32] As underlined by Hix and Høyland, the Commission's organization is comparable to that of a domestic government: Whereas the College of Commissioners as the 'core executive' concentrates on political tasks, its 33 Directorate-Generals (DGs) focus more on bureaucratic responsibilities, such as drafting legislation. Additionally, the body is assisted by a "network of quasi-autonomous agencies" in charge of monitoring regulatory tasks and administrative work. Moreover, the Commission represents the EU in bilateral and multilateral trade negotiations.[33] Led by 28 commissioners, the work of the Commission is furthermore supported by a pool of around 30,000 staff, of which 22,000 are serving as officials.[34] Still, the Commission cannot act completely independently when shaping policy outcomes. The Council of Ministers has designed an 'elaborate system of committees' to be composed of national government officials and to serve the idea of creating a dialogue between national agencies, national governments, and the Commission to discuss the feasibility of implementing EU legislation. This system, which is also referred to as 'comitology,' thereby allows the Member States to scrutinize the executive.[35] However, the Commission is not bound to follow the advice of national experts.[36]

2.1.2 Decision-making in the EU

Since the Treaty of Lisbon, a major portion of EU legislation is jointly decided by the EP and the Council through co-legislation in the ordinary legislative procedure. After the EU Commission has drafted a legislative proposal, the latter

---

[29] Europa. (n.d.e). Glossary: European Commission. http://europa.eu/legislation_summaries/glossary/european_commission_en.htm. visited on July 15, 2013.
[30] Naurin, D. (2004). *Dressed for Politics. Why Increasing Transparency in the European Union Will Not Make Lobbyists Behave Any Better Than They Already Do*. Göteborg: Department of Political Science Göteborg, p. 12.
[31] Nugent, N. (^{7}2010). *The Government and Politics of the European Union. The European Union Series*. Houndmills (UK)/New York: Palgrave MacMillan, p. 105.
[32] Europa (n.d.e).
[33] Hix and Høyland (^{3}2011), p. 34.
[34] Commission Representative. (2013b). E-mail received on May 6, 2013.
[35] Hix and Høyland (^{3}2011), p. 37.
[36] Ibid., p. 38.

is transferred for its first reading to the EP before it gets passed on to the Council of Ministers. If no agreement is reached during the first reading, a second one has to take place. The opportunity to reach a compromise already before that is provided through informal trilogues, which involve representatives of the EP, the Council, and the Commission. If the second reading—with or without such a trilogue—does not result in an agreement on the legislation concerned, a conciliation committee can finally try to compromise the views of both. If the latter option also fails, the legislative draft cannot be adopted. While 60 percent of legislative proposals are agreed on in the first reading and 30 percent are accepted by the co-legislators in the second reading, 10 percent still have to pass the conciliation committee.[37] During the legislative procedure, the extent of power of all three institutions according to the particular period varies: As Irina Michalowitz emphasizes, the Commission is most powerful during the phase of formulating a legislative proposal, but its influence diminishes once the proposal is transferred to the EP. Conversely, both the Council of Ministers and the EP have few or no power during the formulation period, but gain influence as soon as the proposal is on their table of debate.[38] Before the EP and the Council will debate a legislative draft, the EU Commission uses **stakeholder dialogues** in the shape of hearings or workshops to gather scientific input on the draft concerned. Depending on the issue, consultations can be joined by "representatives of regional and local authorities, civil society organisations, undertakings and associations of undertakings, the individual citizens concerned, academics and technical experts, and interested parties in third countries."[39] Another consultation tool to stimulate a debate on a legislative issue is formed by **Green Papers**: By asking bodies or individuals to include their ideas into the consultation process, they were designed by the Commission to develop an overview of the regulatory situation of a certain legislative area, examine the need for further measures, discuss the feasibility of a legislative issue, and may result in "legislative developments."[40]

---

[37] Nugent ([7]2010), p. 183.
[38] Michalowitz, I. (2007). Lobbying in der EU. Wien: facultas wuv, p. 177.
[39] Commission of the European Communities. (2002). Communication from the Commission. Towards a reinforced culture of consultation and dialogue—General principles and minimum standards for consultation of interested parties by the Commission. http://eur-lex.europa.eu/LexUriServ/LexUriServ.do?uri=COM:2002:0704:FIN:EN:PDF, visited on July 15, 2013, p. 4.
[40] Europa. (n.d.a). Glossary: Green Paper. http://europa.eu/legislation_summaries/glossary/green_paper_en.htm, visited on May 5, 2013.

On the basis of such prelegislative preparatory papers, **public consultations** can be launched to evoke a discussion: This includes forms as online consultation, open hearings and seminars, ad hoc meetings, consultation of advisory bodies, or panels including small- and medium-sized enterprises. Debates based on such papers can furthermore result in more than one legislative proposal.[41] Only through online consultation, about 130 consultations can be discussed per year.[42] Green Papers can then further result in prelegislative **White Papers** of the Commission, containing proposals for Community action in a certain area. In case such a Paper is 'favorably received' by the Council of Ministers, an action program for the Union may be launched.[43] Once the public consultation procedure is terminated, the legislative draft will be transferred to the EP for its first reading.

Lobbying the European Parliament
As a consequence of the EP's development toward a co-legislator and due to its extended legislative influence, the amount of interest representatives it attracts has also risen.[44] Before any OLP reading can take place and the plenary can hold a vote on the legislative draft of the Commission, the proposal is debated in the responsible committee. In collaboration with his or her committee, a rapporteur is in charge of drafting the committee's report about the legislative draft, which details the particular modification proposals. The rapporteur is furthermore assisted by shadow rapporteurs to assure that the views of every political group in Parliament, and thus the fractions other than the one of the rapporteur, are heard and involved to an appropriate degree. After the report has been debated in the committee and passed its vote, it is transferred to the parliamentary assembly for the final vote on the side of the EP before the issue will be passed on to the Council.[45]

Generally, the EP can be accessed by interest representatives by contacting MEPs and their rapporteurs in particular. Influence can be directed to the EP's seven political groups, especially since whip is nonexistent; and lobbyists can also try to build contacts with the EP's intergroups, being established as

---

[41] EuropeDirect. (2013). E-mail received on August 1, 2013.
[42] Van Schendelen (^{1}2012), p. 82.
[43] Europa (n.d.b). Glossary: White Paper. http://europa.eu/legislation_summaries/glossary/white_paper_en.htm, visited on May 5, 2013.
[44] Nugent (^{7}2010), p. 251.
[45] European Union. (n.d.). Parliamentary Committees. http://europa.eu/legislation_summaries/glossary/parliamentary_committees_en.htm, visited on April 17, 2013.

"loosely organised and voluntary groupings," allowing MEPs from different fractions to debate issues of common concern.[46] As another approach to address one's interest, lobbyists can also attempt to benefit from the impact of domestic party hierarchies on voting.[47] Eising and Lehringer identify especially the 20 standing committees as one of the EP's most important addressees for lobbyists.[48] Since the rapporteur is also allowed to receive information from external experts[49] and is *de facto* the person in charge of the exact wording of the amended legislative draft, it is no surprise that rapporteurs in general are attractive target persons for lobbyists.

Lobbying the Council of the EU
Since the Council is composed of the governments of the Union's Member States, it bundles the Members' national interests at European level.[50] Obviously, perceptions on the 'lobbyability' of the Council of Ministers highly diverge. Rainer Eising describes the institution as "a highly relevant contact for interest groups" even if generally less addressed by the latter and hardly being lobbied directly.[51] This can also be justified by the assumption that first, the Council is not that 'free' in tolerating external influence, and second, as a body representing national governments it is less dependent on additional knowledge on European level than the EP and the Commission.[52] Moreover, Hans-Wolfgang Platzer argued that due to the Council's complicated procedure of intergovernmental bargaining and administrative cooperation, the institution is also 'shielded' from direct influence of associations.[53] In case political influence is still intended, it is mainly national groups[54] that directly address national ministers or permanent representatives based in Brussels.[55]

---

[46] Nugent ([7]2010), p. 251.
[47] Richardson, J. ([3]2006). *European Union. Power and Policy-making*. Abingdon, Oxon: Routledge, p. 149.
[48] Eising (2010), p. 192.
[49] European Parliament. (2006). A 'Rapporteur'—The Person Who Presents Reports to Parliament. http://www.europarl.europa.eu/sides/getDoc.do?type=IM-PRESS&reference=20060725STO09938&language=EN, visited on April 17, 2013.
[50] Klüver, H. (2012). *Interessenvermittlung in der Europäischen Union. Nationale Verbände auf dem Weg nach Brüssel*. Saarbrücken: AV Akademiker Verlag, p. 52.
[51] Eising ([3]2010), p. 192.
[52] Michalowitz (2007), p. 71.
[53] Platzer, H.-W. (2010). "Europäische Arbeitgeber- und Wirtschaftsverbände". In: W. Schroeder and B. Weßels (eds.). *Handbuch Arbeitgeber- und Wirtschaftsverbände in Deutschland*, Wiesbaden: Verlag für Sozialwissenschaften, p. 435.
[54] See also Richardson ([3]2006), p. 263.
[55] Eising (2005), p. 22; see also Richardson, ibid., p. 262.

An additional possibility to present one's interest vis-à-vis the organ is to lobby the national governments themselves or the Council's working groups.[56] Especially these technical experts can be of high importance since they might *de facto* be the only national experts on a certain legislative issue.[57] Moreover, lobbying the Council and COREPER can also be futile in blocking and reformulating a certain policy.[58] As Nugent further explains, especially with regard to technically complicated issues, it is also the Member States' governments consulting 'relevant interests' already at an early point of time during the Council's internal decision process on a legislative issue. As an example for that, the scholar points to the possibility of a direct communication between interest representatives and members of Council working parties, the number of which is currently maintained at 186.[59]

Lobbying the EU Commission
Asserted by Nugent, the EU Commission is the main target for most of the interest representatives addressing Brussels' institutions. To explain this, the scholar points to the Commission's role of initiating, formulating, and finally implementing policy, as well as to its managing responsibility with regard to programs and funding. Apart from that, for an efficient execution of its duties, the Commission needs to include expert knowledge of interest representatives into the preparation of its work.[60] Pieter Bouwen goes even one step further: According to him, the Commission maintains three tools to shape interest representation in the EU—namely, financial resources, rule-making power, and governance style. Thereby, it subordinates some interest groups to certain policy areas and to a major degree determines the character of interest group constellation.[61] For gaining expert knowledge, the Commission officially seeks the advice of its own network of expert groups.[62] Such groups can involve: individ-

---

[56] Richardson, ibid., p. 263.
[57] Official of the Council. (2013a). Interview of April 26, 2013.
[58] Coen, D. and Richardson, J. (2011). *Lobbying the European Union: Institutions, Actors, and Issues.* Oxford: Oxford University Press, p. 11.
[59] Nugent ([7]2010), p. 249f.
[60] Nugent, ibid., p. 250.
[61] Bouwen, P. (2011). The European Commission. In: D. Coen and J. Richardson (eds.), *Lobbying the European Union: Institutions, Actors, and Issues.* Oxford: Oxford University Press, p. 26.
[62] Van Schendelen ([1]2012), p. 83.

uals, regional- and local-level authorities, and organizations such as companies, associations, NGOs, trade unions, or universities.[63] All groups are asked to list themselves in the Commission's Register of Commission Expert Groups. In 2010, 1,400 groups were officially registered, whereas the insider figure stood at approximately 2,000 groups.[64] Apart from 'common' tools of lobbyists to utter their interests through direct communication with Commission's representatives or by the attendance of meetings, further access to the Commission can be achieved through its advisory committee system or interest delegations meeting the Commissioners and DG officials.[65]

2.1.3 Political system of the United States

The political system of the United States is built on the concepts of representative democracy[66] and Federalism, since the national government shares powers with its 50 single states and the Federal state (District of Columbia[67]) and incorporates the assembly of Congress.[68] The Congress itself is divided into the Senate, which is composed of two representatives for each state and, therefore, 100 members rotating every six years, and the House of Representatives, involving 435 members serving their duty for a two-year term.[69] Therefore, a Congress term lasts only two years. Whereas the House of Representatives covers the political will of the US population, the Senate represents interests of the single states.[70]

The US constitution determines that Congress (Legislative), the President (Executive), as well as US Courts (Judicative) form a system of separate institutions. By enabling these three governmental branches to share and, therefore,

---

[63] Europa. (n.d.f). Register of Commission Expert Groups and other Similar Entities. Expert Groups explained. http://ec.europa.eu/transparency/regexpert/index.cfm?do=faq.faq&aide=2, visited on June 1, 2013.
[64] Van Schendelen ([1]2012), p. 83; unfortunately, the file on the current number of registration was not accessible; however, it was assumed that the amount of 2010 resembles the numbers of 2013.
[65] Nugent ([7]2010), p. 251.
[66] Wilson, J.Q. et al. ([12]2011). American Government. Institutions and Policies. Boston: Cengage Learning, p. 8.
[67] Ibid., p. 52.
[68] Ibid., p. 314.
[69] Ibid., p. 349.
[70] Haas, C.M. et al. ([3]2007). Der Kongreß. In: W. Jäger et al. (eds.), Regierungssystem der USA. Lehr- und Handbuch. München: Oldenbourg Wissenschaftsverlag GmbH, p. 102.

scrutinize their powers, the system is also referred to as "checks and balances."[71] As Martin Sebaldt points out, in practice this system has led to a fascinating power game between the Congress and the President. Even if a distinctive institutional division of powers does exist between the directly elected Chief Executive and the Congress, political routine forces them to permanently cooperate, especially with regard to legislative authority. Where the Congress is endowed with the exclusive right for legislative initiative, the President is still able to apply his or her effective veto right.[72] As a matter of principle, the approach of checks and balances is also reflected by the design of the single states, since all of them possess their own legislative assembly, executive organs, and 'supreme' courts,[73] and are based on their own state constitutions. Consequently, every state is led by its own government. In the United States, like in the EU, legislative competences can be exclusive or shared.

Wienand Gellner and Martin Kleiber identify the US Congress as an example for a working parliament where legislative work is preceded in committees. Similar to interest groups, lobbyists, and executive agencies, Congress committees apply their instrument of aggregation of interests and form a necessary part within the US system due to their legislative monopoly of initiative.[74] Influence of political parties is limited by committee votes, since fractions tend to remain rather hesitant in pushing voting with respect to their party line, but are primarily concerned about voting according to their voters' needs. Therefore, the authors also describe such committees as "classical gate keepers."[75] Due to the increase of external policy-related interest groups since the 1980s, the dimension of scrutiny on the government has broadened. Most lobby groups monitor governmental policies precisely and endow the Congress with necessary information in the event of irregularities. As Gellner and Klieber assume, without this contribution, the Congress would be overstrained with scrutinizing the Executive on its own.[76]

---

[71] Wilson (^{12}2011), p. 31.
[72] Sebaldt, M. (^{1}2007). Strukturen des Lobbying: Deutschland und die USA im Vergleich. In: R. Kleinfeld et al. (eds.), *Lobbying. Strukturen. Akteure. Strategien.* Wiesbaden: VS Verlag für Sozialwissenschaften, p. 104.
[73] Gellner, W. and Kleiber, M. (^{1}2007). *Das Regierungssystem der USA. Eine Einführung.* Baden-Baden: Nomos Verlagsgesellschaft, p. 32.
[74] Ibid., p. 42.
[75] Ibid., p. 43.
[76] Ibid., p. 59.

2.1.4 Decision-making in the United States

Any member of Congress can introduce a bill, and thereby initiate legislation. Bills can be private, when dealing with specific, private, personal or local matters, or public if related to a general concern.[77] A bill does not necessarily have to be drafted by a member of Congress—as Wilson et al. underline, lobbyists and interest groups can also be the editors of such a draft, for instance.[78] While the President as the Chief Executive can be the principal author of a bill, he or she cannot introduce legislation, and is thus forced to rely on a member of Congress to do so by recommending its introduction.[79] In addition, any bill submitted by the President should have involved consideration by congressional key leaders in advance.[80] A decisive part of legislative work within the US Congress is exercised by committees. Whereas *Standing Committees* are employed by each chamber for a long-term period to discuss bills and to control the Executive, *Joint Committees* are formed by representatives of both Chambers to clarify and solve current problems and responsibilities of common concern. However, they do not have any legislative powers. *Special Committees* are established to work on rather specific topics, such as legislative constitutional barriers. Whereas *Select Committees* function as temporarily installed committees of enquiry, a last category entitled *Conference Committees* serves as ad hoc mediators.[81]

A second form of ad hoc committees can be established by US parties, lobbyists, or representatives of interest groups, Congress experts, think tanks, or nonadministrative experts, who organize themselves in so-called *issue networks*.[82] After a bill has been introduced by a member of Congress and gets numbered, the committee in charge has to decide whether the bill will be passed for further debates or stopped immediately. Therefore, committees of both Congress chambers regularly consult experts in special hearings. By the involvement of experts, such as citizen groups or private individuals, Congress seeks to collect written or oral testimony and evidence regarding a legislative proposal, nominations, or treaties, from anyone with an interest in the bill.[83]

---

[77] Wilson et al. (^{12}2011), p. 341.
[78] Ibid., p. 342; see also Haas (^{3}2007), p. 187.
[79] See also USinfo (n.d.). The President of the United States: Legislative Powers. http://usinfo.org/enus/government/branches/ben_president2.html, visited on July 20, 2013.
[80] Wilson et al. (^{12}2011), p. 341.
[81] Gellner and Kleiber (^{1}2007), p. 43f.
[82] Ibid., pp. 47, 165.
[83] Patrick, J.J. et al. (^{5}2002). *The Oxford Guide to the United States Government*. Oxford: Oxford University Press, hearings, congressional.

Once those hearings are completed, they are followed by so-called 'mark-up' sessions, where members of the responsible committees as well as related subcommittees examine in detail those views presented during the hearings. All amendments to the introduced bill, which have been generated by those hearings, require a vote by the particular committee.[84] As a next step, the bill is passed for 'floor action' to the full assembly of the chamber to which the committee belongs and from which the bill originally derived. After the conclusion of all debates in the assembly, the particular chamber votes on a final passage of the draft. If the bill passes the vote successfully and is not 'recommitted' to the committee in charge, the procedure will repeat itself in the second chamber of Congress. In case the latter decides to amend the bill, the draft requires to be returned to the chamber of the bill's origin. If a joint agreement of both chambers on the bill's exact wording turns out to be difficult to reach, a conference committee as a joint mediator will be appointed. The compromising report of this institution, which comprises members from both chambers, will finally be sent to both the House of Representatives and the Senate for another vote.[85] Once they both agree, it can finally be transferred to the Chief Executive: The US President.

The US law and constitutional amendments can be adopted without the President's sponsorship or signature.[86] Generally, the President can choose from three options: to approve the bill and sign it; to veto it; or not to act at all. Once a bill is signed by the President and implemented into law, only the Supreme Court can declare it unconstitutional and defeat it. By a President's veto the bill is sent back to Congress unsigned. However, the Congress can still 'override' the veto by a two-third majority of each chamber in favor of the bill.[87] According to the third option, if Congress conducts a sitting 10 business days after the President's reception of the bill, the latter will be amended without the President to sign it. Alternatively, the bill can 'die' in case a Congress sitting is not sum-

---

[84] United States House of Representatives. (n.d.) The Legislative Process. http://www.house.gov/content/learn/legislative_process/, visited on July 20, 2013.
[85] United States House of Representatives. (n.d.) The Legislative Process. http://www.house.gov/content/learn/legislative_process/, visited on July 20, 2013; "House Floor"; "To the Senate."
[86] Wilson et al. (^{12}2011), p. 342.
[87] Wilson et al. (^{12}2011), p. 342; see also USinfo (n.d.).

moned within the 10-day period after the bill's transferral to the Chief Executive.[88] Despite the existing institutional separation of powers, the political everyday life, therefore, forces both the President as well as the Congress to permanently cooperate.[89]

As Hartmut Wasser points out, especially subcommittees have been implemented to institutionalize interest organization within the policy process. He identifies expert hearings to be a means for improving the efficiency of Congress legislation. Still, the scholar is convinced that the inclusion of lobbyists into such hearings does not reduce the general number of lobbyists influencing Congressmen.[90] As in the EU, members of committees in charge of a bill are those voting on and creating a bill. Thus, it is not surprising that they frequently become targets of lobbyists.[91] As Wilson et al. argue, most of the power in Congress can be assigned to the chairmanships of such committees as well as to their subcommittees.[92] Likewise, the Executive Office of the President is also an attractive addressee for lobbyists to direct their concerns.[93] This is especially related to the fact that already during the initial period of a bill or its reading in the chambers of Congress, the White House can pressurize the Congress by referring to its right of veto.[94] As Rosenthal points out, the "greatest tactical challenge" of a lobbyist is offered during the final days of a session, since additional wording can still be included amid the debate about amendments.[95] Finally, US administration belongs to the main targets of interest groups and associations since its agencies are perceived as very influential and powerful with regard to the execution of law. Likewise, the administration depends on specific topic-related expert knowledge of interest representatives.[96]

---

[88] USinfo, ibid.
[89] Sebaldt, M. (2011). *Transformation der Verbändedemokratie. Die Modernisierung des Systems organisierter Interessen in den USA*. Wiesbaden: Westdeutscher Verlag GmbH, p. 69.
[90] Wasser, H. (^{3}2007). Interessengruppen. In: W. Jäger et al. (eds.), *Regierungssystem der USA. Lehr- und Handbuch*. München: Oldenbourg Wissenschaftsverlag GmbH, p. 339.
[91] Gellner and Kleiber (^{1}2007), p. 47.
[92] Wilson et al. (^{12}2011), p. 336.
[93] Berry, J.M. (^{3}1997). *The Interest Group Society*. NL: Longman, p. 173.
[94] Gellner and Kleiber (^{1}2007), p. 48.
[95] Rosenthal, A. (1993). *The Third House. Lobbyists and Lobbying in the States*. Washington, DC: Congressional Quarterly Inc., p. 189.
[96] Wasser (^{3}2007), p. 336.

2.2 Influencing political decision-making

2.2.1 Lobbying

Although perceived by lobbyists themselves as an ideal strategy to push forward interests and make one's view heard during political decision-making, lobbying is regarded from a rather suspicious angle among society. Especially in Brussels and Washington, DC, numbers of lobbyists have steadily been growing—as a result, not only the public but also politicians strive for measures to deal with this seemingly unlimited resource of external information and influence in an attempt to make the profession of lobbying more transparent. This chapter defines lobbying and contrasts concepts of interest representation applied in the EU and the United States, respectively. Further, terms such as regulation, register, interest groups, and transparency will be specified in detail. However, as science has still not agreed on a common definition of lobbying, framing the scope of the term remains imperfect in the chapter at hand.

The origination of the term "lobby" can be traced back to the mid-16th century when it was first used as part of the English vocabulary for the entrance hall and corridors of the English House of Commons. Furthermore, it is related to the Latin word "labium," which refers to an entrance or waiting hall. From 1832 onwards, lobbying in the United States was defined as applying illegitimate methods of corruption and bribery to represent one's interests. Interest group representatives were entitled "lobbyists" after the White House had temporarily moved to a hotel during the presidency of Ulysses S. Grant (1869–1877), and such group representatives used to wait in the hotel's lobby so they could speak with the White House staff.[97] Even today, lobbyists seek to influence the political decision-making process at the legislative, executive, and judicative level, and address their interests to communal, regional, national, and supranational powers.[98] The Organisation for Economic Co-operation and Development (OECD) officially defines lobbying as "the oral or written communication with a public official to influence legislation, policy or administrative decisions" directed toward the legislative and executive branch to influence adoptions of legislation, projects, and contract design.[99] Both their aims to reach political

---

[97] Kraft, E. (2006). *Lobbying in der EU. Regulierung nach US-Vorbild?* Saarbrücken: VDM Verlag Dr. Müller, pp. 18f.

[98] Brockhaus, der. (2008). *Politik. Ideen, Systeme und Prozesse.* Mannheim: F.A. Brockhaus, p. 273.

[99] OECD. (2010a). Recommendation of the Council on Principles for Transparency and Integrity in Lobbying. http://acts.oecd.org/Instruments/ShowInstrumentView.aspx?InstrumentID=256&InstrumentPID=%20250, visited on January 16, 2014.

goals as well as to build coalitions are considered by scholars as the two main targets of lobbyists when establishing and maintaining contacts with political leaders and other interest representatives.[100] By that, lobbyists strive to make themselves visible and heard by politicians.[101] Thus, a successful lobbyist needs to be credible, effective, and reliable. Beyond that, he or she should be endowed with good judgment as well as the ability to evoke empathy and a durable relationship with legislators.[102] Being a lobbyist requires attentive monitoring of the decision-making process to gather relevant information as early as possible and be updated at any time. Necessarily, a lobbyist should identify key decision-makers and thus the relevant target persons during a legislative procedure. As a matter of principle, lobbying is perceived as a long-term activity.[103]

The classic model of interest groups as part of democratic systems can generally be identified as a tool to serve the concept of pluralism: Identified by Hix and Høyland, the central idea behind this model is open access for private citizens and organized groups toward policy makers creating a system of "checks and balances against powerful state officials." In addition, for each political group and attitude a contrary one can be found.[104] Whereas the concept of lobbying can be subordinated to the broad field of public affairs management,[105] it is also regarded as an exchange: To increase the success of their influence, lobbyists always need to be able to offer return favors to politicians and civil servants. According to the concept of "do ut des,"[106] this could be information, monetary contributions, or votes, for instance.[107] Especially, the exchange of information needs to be timely and accurate.[108] Gathering and bundling information through coalition-building has also become one of the major

---

[100] Ainsworth, S. (^{1}2010). Methodological Perspectives on Interest Groups. In: L.S. Maisel and J.M. Berry (eds.), *The Oxford Handbook of American Political Parties and Interest Groups*. New York: Oxford University Press Inc., p. 89.
[101] Berry (^{3}1997), p. 96.
[102] Rosenthal (1993), p. 122.
[103] Prenzel, T. (2007). *Handbuch Lobbyarbeit konkret*. Schwalbach: WOCHENSCHAU Verlag, p. 12.
[104] Hix and Høyland (^{3}2011), p. 159.
[105] Van Schendelen (^{1}2012), p. VII.
[106] "I give so that you might give" (translated from Latin).
[107] Buholzer (1998), p. 129.
[108] Salisbury, R.H. (^{2}1990). The Paradox of Interest Groups in Washington—More Groups, less Clout. In: A. King et al. (eds.), *The New American Political System*. Lanham, Maryland: University Press of America Inc., p. 226.

tasks of contemporary lobbyists in striving for the most efficacious effort to influence,[109] such as by national or international associations.

According to Eising and Lehringer, European associations in particular intend to influence EU bodies, whereas national associations rather focus on persuading national members of such bodies. As argued, European interest groups are more visible than national ones,[110] while the latter clearly dominate domestic policy areas at Member State level.[111] The modus operandi of lobbyists can furthermore be categorized into **inside- and outside-lobbying**. Whereas an inside-lobbyist tries to communicate directly with a target person, outside lobbying can be described as an indirect attempt to influence the surrounding of political leaders, other relevant opinion leaders, or public opinion. Thus, outside lobbyists seek to communicate public support to policy makers and to strengthen such public support among constituencies.[112] This can also be achieved through mediators, such as mass media, for example. Outside lobbying is also referred to as **grassroots lobbying**. As an example of this tactic applied in the United States, Craig Holman names "public opinion campaigns that encourage citizens to contact Congress about pending legislation."[113] Pointed out by the In-House Lobbyist, grassroots lobbying is based on emotionalizing a certain issue and requires a society where such tools are fruitful. Whereas the US society responded to such measures to a major degree, in Brussels, grassroots lobbying was simply more difficult to realize.[114]

The profession of lobbying is mainly conducted by **in-house lobbyists, associations, lobby organizations, and lobbying firms**. Whereas the latter are simply paid by a client for exerting commercial lobbying activities[115] on a certain target, lobbyists of associations represent a whole range of interests and, thus, have to compromise on various views and needs. Representatives of organizations can either influence politics for a single organization striving for a single interest, or can lobby for an entity that bundles again various interests of members or subentities and is similar to associations. Since associations and lobby

---

[109] Rosenthal (1993), p. 150; Berry (^{3}1997), p. 116; see also Prenzel (2007), p. 10.
[110] Eising and Lehringer (^{3}2010), p. 198.
[111] Ibid., p. 202.
[112] Kollman, K. (1998). *Outside Lobbying. Public Opinion & Interest Group Strategies.* Princeton, NJ: Princeton University Press, p. xiii.
[113] Holman, C. (2008). Making the U.S. Lobbying Disclosure Act Work as Intended: Implications for the European Transparency Initiative. http://www.citizen.org/documents/Making-LDA-Work.pdf, visited on May 18, 2013, p. 4.
[114] In-House Lobbyist. (2013). Interview of June 14, 2013.
[115] Michalowitz (2007), p. 73.

organizations both exercise collective interest representation,[116] they are examples for **interest groups**, which will be defined in detail in Chapter 2.2.2. In-house lobbyists are employed by one actor only; those are usually companies seeking to push forward their particular interest.[117] Since they are not primarily bound to an association, Irina Michalowitz describes in-house lobbyists as more target oriented with regard to their operations.[118] Also commercial consultancies cannot be left out of consideration: Having become a serious actor in the Brussels lobbying business in particular, such agencies are generally engaged in public affairs and offer their services to a variety of clients, such as private sector enterprises, governmental institutions, associations, or NGOs.[119]

But why is lobbying necessary for democracy at all? There is no doubt that political leaders essentially need to gain access to **high-quality information for effective governance.**[120] For the inclusion of the most broad interest variety possible, the political process requires procedures by which an active participation of interest groups is maintained.[121] This is furthermore necessary, since politicians, due to their wide array of topics, simply cannot always provide scientific expert knowledge, which is adequate to judge legislative issues concerned. The survey results of René Paul Buholzer reflect this assumption: 46 percent of lobbyists, politicians, and public servants that had been interviewed agreed that the existence of lobbyists is justifiable by the fact that the expertise of decision-makers is not always sufficient. Even 49 percent supported the idea that lobbying enhances the **prevention from possible bureaucratic mistakes or development of noncomprehensible laws.**[122]

The Commission Representative affirms that creating legislation for 28 Member States makes it impossible to know all details and foresee all impacts of legislation in advance. Thus, lobbyists form a necessary part within the 'wheelwork' of democratic processes.[123] As Buholzer argues with regard to the EU Commission in particular, lobbyists by that can **strengthen the efficiency** of an institution, and **mobilize acceptance** as well as **legitimacy** for a legislative

---

[116] Ibid., p. 78.
[117] Ibid., p. 88.
[118] Michalowitz (2007), p. 90.
[119] Lahusen, C. (^{1}2005). Kommerzielle Beratungsfirmen in der Europäischen Union. In: R. Eising and B. Kohler-Koch (eds.), *Interessenpolitik in Europa. Regieren in Europa 7.* Baden-Baden: Nomos, p. 251.
[120] See Ainsworth, S. (^{1}2010), p. 92; Nugent (^{7}2010), p. 252.
[121] Prenzel (2007), p. 10.
[122] Buholzer (1998), p. 223.
[123] Commission Representative. (2013a). Interview of May 2, 2013.

draft. Likewise, especially interest groups serve as a **connecting link to the public**.[124] In addition, by their expert knowledge and informative resources lobbyists possess influential power, which cannot be underrated. Hence, in addition to the Executive, Legislative, and Judicative branches as well as the media they might even be identified as a fifth power within the political decision-making process. Still, all categorizations and characteristics can just provide a very basic overview on those aspects that the scope of lobbying theoretically can embrace. As the EU Lobbying Expert concludes, the nonexistence of "general knowledge of lobbying is not really surprising […], there is also no general empirical theory of chess."[125]

2.2.2 Interest groups

Defining interest groups requires clarification of the term 'interests' as well. A common distinction by political science literature is outlined by Irina Michalowitz who differentiates between the subcategories of *economic* and *public interests*. Whereas the latter alludes to interests of the common wealth, such as environmental-, employment-, or consumer protection, economic interests strive for saving a certain benefit.[126] Being usually more difficult to organize and push through, public interests are considered as rather the weak interests.[127] Likewise, they are categorized as diffuse.[128] The origination of new interests is a consequence of a society's maturity. Governmental operations necessarily include cooperation and competition among groups that represent such interests.[129] With respect to the United States, interest groups are also referred to as 'pressure groups' to underline the method of pressurizing a target to gain political influence. However, this expression comes along with a rather negative connotation.[130]

To put it simply, interest groups refer to organizations with the intention to influence government.[131] Lobbying activities begin as soon as such a group

---

[124] Buholzer (1998), p. 226.
[125] Van Schendelen, R. (1993). *National Public and Private EC Lobbying*. Aldershot: Dartmouth, p. 14; quoted in: Buholzer (1998), p. 25.
[126] Michalowitz (2007), pp. 51f., see also Eising and Lehringer (^{3}2010), pp. 192, 200; Berry (1997), p. 31.
[127] Michalowitz (2007), p. 52.
[128] Eising and Lehringer (^{3}2010), pp. 192, 200.
[129] Grossmann, M. (2012). *The Not-So-Special Interests. Interest Groups, Public Representation, and American Governance*. Stanford, CA: Stanford University Press, p. 11.
[130] Kraft (2006), p. 9.
[131] Berry (1997), pp. 4f.

starts exercising influence on policy makers in a certain field.[132] Amid growing tendencies of individualization and pluralism among societies, interest groups and organizations essentially function as a **medium to bundle and convey interests** between the state and its citizens. Thus, they can either be perceived as some kind of **second level of representation** within the representative-political system, or as a **primary horizontal connection between state and society**.[133] Moreover, they are characterized as one of the **most vital elements of civil participation and interest procurement** within the political process,[134] while committing themselves for their own political agenda and for monitoring the political development.[135] Eising even defines them as indispensable "schools for democracy" with socialized citizens as political beings.

On the other hand, they can also be shaped by political institutions with regard to their formation, role, function, and strategies to influence political decisions.[136] Interest groups can be composed of lobbies, pressure groups, NGOs, social movement organizations, and interest organizations.[137] Furthermore, associations can also form an interest group. Particularly active in the EU, the main tasks of associations are bundling information to a common position and representing the latter, opening channels of access to the European institutions, transferring information to its members, external representation within the formation of public opinion, and finally implementing European measures.[138] The discussion about interest groups and lobbying also involves the term "stakeholder." A stakeholder can both be a person or an entity representing certain interests and influencing the outcome of interest representation. Thus, an interest group can also be referred to as a stakeholder.[139]

2.2.3 History of lobbying regulation in the EU

The involvement of interest groups into the EU's political decision-making is a tradition that can be traced back to the origin of the EU. The Treaty establishing the European Coal and Steel Community (ECSC) in 1952 allowed the former High Authority, which is now the Commission, to hear associations and experts

---

[132] Eising and Lehringer (^{3}2010), p. 191.
[133] Kraft (2006), p. 12; Berry (1997), pp. 6f.
[134] Berry (1997) pp. 6f.
[135] Ibid., p. 8.
[136] Eising and Lehringer (^{3}2010), p. 191. p. 203.
[137] Ibid, p. 191.
[138] Eising and Kohler-Koch (^{1}2005), p. 29.
[139] Van Schendelen (^{1}2012), pp. 188f.

at any time.[140] Simultaneously, the foundation of the ECSC in 1952 as well as the establishment of the European Economic Community and the European Atomic Energy Community in 1958 led to an increase in European association structures.[141] According to Woll, the number of European associations grew ninefold since the 1950s.[142] In the EU, lobbying of political leaders by private firms at national level started in the 1970s and 1980s[143]. As Ahrens critically underlines, the need for a lobbying regulation in the EU mainly derived from an 'evolution' of lobbying after the introduction of the internal market program in 1986: A volatile growth of lobbying activities and a change in lobbying tactics caused a capacity overload of the decision-making procedure.[144]

In his privately published report "The Ghost of Brussels" of 1991, the Dutch MEP Alman Metten observed a lack of transparency and balance in EU lobbying and suggested a register and a code of conduct for interest representatives. His proposition attracted media attention and led to the first EP hearing on lobbying in 1992.[145] As a consequence, the Commission proposed a code of conduct binding lobbyists to disclose their interests and to desist from offering incentives as well as from disseminating misleading information.[146] Furthermore, the Commission proposed an "open and structured dialogue" between interest representatives and political leadership.[147] Alternatively, Metten convinced the EP to develop first regulations in shape of a register for interest groups in 1996[148] and to establish a code of conduct in 1997 for lobbyists that were accredited by the EP. In the meantime, the Commission and the Council also designed a similar code for staff and outsiders and started distributing registration forms.[149] As registration and the acceptance of the code of conduct were linked to the distribution of passes for a simplified accessibility of the EP, this register can be identified as the 'predecessor' of the TR.

---

[140] Weidenfeld, W. and Wessel, W. (eds.). 2011. *Europa von A bis Z. Schriftenreihe*, Band 1123. Bonn: Bundeszentrale für politische Bildung, p. 361.
[141] Kraft (2006), p. 35.
[142] Woll, C. (2006). Research agenda. Lobbying in the European Union: From sui generis to a comparative perspective. *Journal of European Public Policy*, 2006, **13** (3), p. 2.
[143] Hix and Høyland (^{3}2011), p. 165.
[144] Ahrens, K. (^{1}2007). Nutzen und Grenzen der Regulierung von Lobbying. In: R. Kleinfeld Ralf et al. (eds.), *Lobbying. Strukturen. Akteure. Strategien*. Wiesbaden: VS Verlag für Sozialwissenschaften, p. 125.
[145] Van Schendelen (2012), p. 385.
[146] Weidenfeld and Wessel (2011), p. 363.
[147] Eising and Lehringer (^{3}2010), p. 194.
[148] Eising and Kohler-Koch (^{1}2005), p. 23.
[149] Van Schendelen (2012), p. 385.

However, even if registrants' names were publicly visible on the EP website, other relevant information, such as their field of interest and legislative targets, remained unrevealed.[150] In 2001, the Commission launched a White Paper on European Governance, including the launch of its own web-based expert register and a comprehensive code of practice for those providing and receiving expert knowledge. As a consequence, the Commission adopted a set of principles and standards to generally improve transparency of consultations with interest groups.[151] Presented by the former Administrative Affairs, Audit and Anti-fraud Commissioner Siim Kallas[152], the Commission launched the first ETI in 2005[153] to improve registration, tighten rules of conduct for lobbyists, and to regain trust of EU citizens in transparent decision-making.[154] According to Gentili, the ETI can also be described as a personal initiative of Commissioner Kallas whose "driving force" consisted of an informal cooperation between the EU Commission itself and NGOs, such as ALTER-EU.[155] Originally, Kallas had intended an obligatory system of disclosure; however, against the advice of various experts and NGOs, he had to announce that the Commission's register to be launched in 2008 would be voluntary.[156] The Commission assessed this solution more 'appropriate' since the institution itself lacked essential watchdog powers and favored a nonrestrictive definition of lobbying.[157] In 2008, the Commission launched its own voluntary "Register of Interest Representatives" (ROIR),[158] which in June 2011 amounted to 4,000 registrants.[159] The implementation of two different registers in the past can be explained by the fact that

---

[150] Holman, C. and Luneburg, W. (2012). Lobbying and Transparency: A Comparative Analysis of Regulatory Reform. http://www.palgrave-journals.com/iga/journal/v1/n1/full/iga20124a.html, visited on April 28, 2013.
[151] Eising and Lehringer (^{3}2010), pp. 194f.
[152] Ibid., p. 195.
[153] Europa. (2012). First Annual Report on Transparency Register shows good start, and sets further objectives for 2013. http://europa.eu/rapid/press-release_IP-12-1265_en.htm, visited on July 12, 2013.
[154] The EU Watchdog Representative. (2013a). Interview of April 25, 2013.
[155] Gentili (2013), p. 5.
[156] Arte+7. (n.d.) The Brussels Business. http://www.youtube.com/watch?v=60xbEoDQ4RM, visited on March 2, 2013.
[157] Gentili (2013), p. 6.
[158] ALTER-EU. (2012). Dodgy Data. Time to Fix the EU's Transparency Register. http://www.alter-eu.org/sites/default/files/documents/Dodgy-data.pdf, visited on May 19, 2013, p. 4.
[159] Šefčovič, M. (2011). Lobbyismus braucht Transparenz. Das neue Transparenz-Register des Europäischen Parlaments und der Europäischen Kommission. In: "Recht und Politik", Ausgabe 04/2011, Berlin: Berliner Wirtschaftsverlag. http://ec.europa.eu/commission_2010-2014/sefcovic/headlines/articles/2011/12/index_en.htm, visited on May 21, 2013, pp. 198f.

both institutions sought to maintain a certain degree of autonomy in regulating their operational rules, and that there was no underlying obligation to synchronize registers.[160]

Interestingly, in April 2008, the EP had already initiated a motion for a resolution that included a call for a mandatory register common to all three institutions that was adopted in May.[161] General negotiations about a joint register started in Spring 2010.[162] On June 23, 2011, the Inter-Institutional Relations and Administration Commissioner Maroš Šefčovič eventually launched the TR, which was based on an Interinstitutional Agreement (IIA) signed by the EP and the European Commission.[163] Not only was the TR a totally new type of register for the EU, but so was its secretariat, the JTRS, which is operated by two employees of each institution and introduces "a new and innovative work format within the EU's institutions."[164] According to the EU watchdog representative, during the preparation phase of the TR especially lobby groups opposed themselves to a mandatory concept: They feared that the disclosure of information about their strategy or sensitive commercial data might be an advantage for their competitors.[165] The reason why the TR is not entitled 'lobby register' is based on the fact that it not only does address pure lobbyists, but also anyone intending to influence the decision-making process.[166] In comparison to ROIR, Commissioner Šefčovič presented the TR as "a better service [...] characterised by greater transparency, accessibility, and more detailed information on registrants."

Furthermore, the scope of registrants was widened by the inclusion of law firms, NGOs, and think tanks.[167] Both the TR and the JTRS commenced operations on July 1, 2011. The JTRS is subordinated to the Unit for Transparency and Relations with Interest Groups in the Secretariat-General of the European Commission, with Gérard Legris as its head, as well as to the Transparency

---

[160] Obradovic, D. (2011). Regulating Lobbying in the European Union. In: D. Coen and J. Richardson (eds.), *Lobbying the European Union: Institutions, Actors, and Issues*. Oxford: Oxford University Press, p. 318.
[161] ALTER-EU (2012), p. 4.
[162] Šefčovič (2011), p. 199.
[163] Europa. (2011b). Parliament Magazine, "*Open for Business.*" http://ec.europa.eu/commission_2010-2014/sefcovic/documents/022-025_parliament_27_june.pdf, visited on May 5, 2013, p. 22.
[164] Europa (2012).
[165] EU Watchdog Representative (2013a).
[166] Commission Representative. (2013b). E-mail received on May 6, 2013.
[167] Europa (2011c).

Unit of the DG Presidency of the Parliament, headed by Jose Rufas. ROIR registrants were transferred to the TR within a 12-month period.[168] In March 2012, a new electronic system for EP accreditation was linked to the register, which replaced the previous paper-based accreditation.

To intensify cooperation between the EU's key institutions in the framework of the TR, from June 2012 onwards, a member of the GSC started participating in the weekly meetings of the JTRS as an informative observer.[169] The latter reports regularly to the Council and familiarizes the GSC with the system of the TR.[170] The Council as well as the European Council are explicitly invited by the IIA to join the EP and the Commission in operating the TR. Moreover, the TR is designed to function as a reference tool for all other institutions, bodies, and agencies of the EU.[171] The Commission Representative assumes possible reasons as to why the Council has not agreed to complement the list of cooperators yet: that the body might be afraid of increased bureaucracy and implications for its own resources, or simply that it does not see "the additional value."[172]

The GSC Representative argues that the institution is to a lesser degree concerned by lobbying activities covered by the register since most contacts between interest groups and the Council occur within national structures, such as in the capitals or permanent representations of Member States.[173] Conversely, ALTER-EU expects substantive lobbying to happen around meetings of the Council as well and enhances the body to become another operator of the TR.[174] Generally, the position of the institution about endowing its General Sec-

---

[168] Europa. (2011c). Commission and European Parliament launch Joint Transparency Register to shed light on all those seeking to influence European policy", Press Release. http://europa.eu/rapid/press-release_IP-11-773_en.htm?locale=en, visited on July 19, 2013.
[169] JTRS. (2012b). Annual Report on the operations of the Transparency Register. http://ec.europa.eu/transparencyregister/info/about-register/reportsAndPublications.do?locale=en, visited on January 15, 2014, 1.1.
[170] Ibid., p. 5.
[171] Official Journal of the European Union. (2011). Interinstitutional Agreement. Agreement between the European Parliament and the European Commission on the establishment of a transparency register for organisations and self-employed individuals engaged in EU policy-making and policy implementation. http://eur-lex.europa.eu/LexUriServ/LexUriServ.do?uri=OJ:L:2011:191:0029:0038:EN:PDF, visited on May 1, 2013, p. VIII.
[172] Commission Representative (2013a).
[173] GSC Representative. (2013). E-mail received on May 15, 2013.
[174] EU Watchdog Representative. (2013b). E-mail received on May 6, 2013.

retariat with this responsibility evolved during the last years: After it had previously insisted on the opinion that it was less lobbied than the EP and the Commission,[175] in 2011 the Council expressed its interest in accepting the invitation to join the TR.[176]

Commissioner Šefčovič describes the TR as "de facto mandatory" since registration is a precondition for the distribution of EP access badges and for engaging in "any serious discussion with the institutions."[177] In addition, fast-track accession is a remarkable ease for the daily work of interest representatives in Brussels and Strasbourg.[178] As the Commission Representative explains, the "*de facto* mandatory" TR is intended to create an atmosphere that makes registration unavoidable for "reasons of good reputation."[179] In June 2013, an Interinstitutional Working Group was launched to debate possible changes of the TR in the context of its revision procedure.[180] While the TR is operated at supranational level, Germany (1972), Poland (1992), Lithuania (2001), France (2009), Slovenia (2011), Austria (2012),[181] and Denmark (2012)[182] also implemented legislation to regulate interest representatives. Recent debates about new instruments of lobbying regulation have taken place in Bulgaria, Croatia, the Czech Republic, Estonia, Ireland, Italy, Latvia, Romania, and the United Kingdom.[183]

Irrespective of lobbying at the Member State level, the stark increase of lobbying activities in Brussels resulted in the city being entitled the "second biggest lobbying industry in the world" by Olivier Hoedeman (Corporate Europe Observatory).[184] Additionally, Buholzer even referred to it as a "true Lobbying-Mekka."[185] Generally, this reflects the increased interest representation in the

---

[175] Council of the European Union. (2008). "I" Item Note, 11374/08. Approval of a reply to the letter of Mr Hans-Gert Pöttering, President of the European Parliament. http://register.con silium.europa.eu/pdf/en/08/st11/st11374.en08.pdf, visited on May 18, 2013.
[176] Official Journal of the European Union (2011), VIII, (28).
[177] Europa (2011c), p. 25.
[178] Šefčovič (2011), p. 201.
[179] Commission Representative (2013a).
[180] ALTER-EU (2012), p. 4.
[181] JTRS (2012b), p. 15, 3.3.2.
[182] LobbyPedia. (2013). Lobbyregister (Überblick). https://lobbypedia.de/wiki/Lobbyregis ter_%28%C3%9Cberblick%29#D.C3.A4nemark, visited on August 9, 2013.
[183] Greenwood, J. and Dreger, J. (2013). The Transparency Register: A European vanguard of strong lobby regulation? http://www.palgrave-journals.com/iga/journal/v2/n2/full/iga20133a.html, visited on August 9, 2013.
[184] Arte+7 (n.d.).
[185] Buholzer (1998), p. 11.

EU since its origin. After the establishment of the EP's lobby register in 1996 and the ROIR in 2008, the TR as a new and innovative work format can be identified as the second level of interest regulation in the EU, which furthermore welcomes the accession of the Council or the European Council as additional operators.

2.2.4 Lobbying in the EU

The White Paper of the European Commission, which was published in 2001, explicitly designates a broad participation of the civil society in the European political process. Complementary to representative democracy, participatory democracy is also laid down in the Treaty of Lisbon. By that, the role of societal organizations and interest groups as part of the European political process gets its constitutional legitimation.[186] Interest representation at European level is characterized by its **multilevel structure**, the central role played by its **system of committees**, a **technical-factual style of politics**, its **accessibility**, as well as **openness** vis-à-vis interest groups.[187]

By that, the multilevel system of the EU also demands multilevel coordination of interest groups across all levels. This complexity also attenuates direct influence of powerful interest groups.[188] Pursuant to Eising and Kohler-Koch, interest groups play a rather consulting role, which might not only be informal and ad hoc, but can also be institutionalized and similar to those of an association.[189] At the EU level it is possible for interest representatives to influence the direction of a certain policy at any stage in the legislative procedure: from its preparation to amendments during adoption, through the postadoption implementation phase to judicial adjudication.[190] With respect to the EU, lobbyists' informative resources can be subdivided into **expert knowledge**, **information on comprehensive European interests**, and **information on comprehensive national interests**.[191]

---

[186] Platzer, H.-W. (2008). Interessenverbände und europäischer Lobbyismus. In: W. Weidenfeld (ed.), Die Europäische Union. Politisches System und Politikbereiche. Bonn: Bundeszentrale für politische Bildung, p. 187.
[187] Klüver (2012), p. 52.
[188] Woll (2005), p. 6.
[189] Eising (^{1}2005), p. 23.
[190] Hix and Høyland (^{3}2011), p. 181.
[191] Bouwen, P. (^{1}2005) Zugangslogik in der Europäischen Union: Der Fall des Europäischen Parlaments. In: R. Eising and B. Kohler-Koch (eds.), Interessenpolitik in Europa. Regieren in Europa 7. Baden-Baden: Nomos, p. 98; Comprehensive interests here refer to the formulation of an interest by several parties.

The inclusion of interest groups' expert knowledge in the EU's policy-making is also referred to as "insourcing" by van Schendelen, who defines this strategy as an administrative culture of consulting.[192] Since this approach is considered as "quite unique," the scholar has entitled it the "Brussels method."[193] Apart from that, van Schendelen categorizes three different routes for lobbyists to 'enter' the complex of the EU: First, they can use the **national route** via national associations; second, by using the **transnational route**, lobbyists can pass their affairs via intrastate associations or via a European Federation directly to the EU; and third, the **international route** allows for transporting interests through international organizations or those of other Member States and third states, respectively.[194] As the EU Lobbying Expert explains, the most applied route by quantity is the direct national route. However, the most efficient approach is to talk to "befriended stakeholders from other countries" before addressing the EU with a "greater weight."[195] As a matter of principle, EU interest groups need to monitor both the supranational as well as the national state level.

As pointed out by Buholzer, interest representation in the EU is articulated in a specific level order: While single interests form the **micro level** as the bottom stage, sectoral interests are referred to as the **meso level**, followed by the **macro level** that represents European associations of national umbrella organizations.[196] Such European associations are also referred to as Euro groups.[197] Especially the EU's multilevel shape provides an increased number of access points to the European decision process for national interests in particular. Consequently, national associations, for instance, can try to conduct their own lobbying activities at the supranational level, but can also benefit from indirect lobbying via transnational European associations.[198] Despite this, direct EU lobbying by large-scale enterprises as well as their common action during EU decision-making processes have increased in reach and quality during the past two decades.[199] Likewise, law firms and consultancies have increased the amount of lobbying on request.[200] However, interest groups in the

---

[192] Van Schendelen (2012), p. 81.
[193] Ibid., p. 84.
[194] Ibid., pp. 148f.
[195] EU Lobbying Expert. (2013). E-mail received on June 22, 2013.
[196] Buholzer (1998), p. 204.
[197] Michalowitz (2007), p. 79.
[198] Klüver (2012), p. 22.
[199] Platzer (2008), p. 200.
[200] Weidenfeld and Wessel (2011), pp. 360f.

shape of associations are still the most important form of interest representation at the European level with respect to economic as well as public interest;[201] during the last years their role in Brussels has been strengthened. This can also be explained by the fact that the EP is formed by international coalitions of national fractions. Contrary to the national level, the institution does not have to build a government and can arguably act more subject-focused.[202] Beyond this, European interest representation in general has steadily been professionalized since the 1980s.[203] Regarding the development within the spectrum of European interest groups, and the boom of commercial consultancies, single representations, and agencies in particular, Kraft even speaks of an "Americanization" in Brussels.[204] Eising and Lehringer estimate that about two-third of EU interest organizations are federations of national interest groups.[205] Apart from that, the authors assume that individual firms have even better access to EU and domestic political institutions than European or national associations would.[206]

A survey conducted by the BM consultancy in 2012 among 600 MEPs, Members of Parliament (MPs) and senior officials from national parliaments or other European institutions divulged the following results. What European policy makers found most positive about lobbying was that it ensured the "participation of social and economic actors and citizens in the political process" (37 percent), and second that lobbyists provided "useful and timely information" (28 percent).[207] Being asked which of the following groups could be considered being 'lobbyists', 86 percent of Brussels-based respondents chose trade associations , 73 percent chose both trade unions and professional organizations, 70 percent chose companies , 68 percent chose NGOs and 66 percent of them chose public affairs agencies.[208]

---

[201] Michalowitz (2007), p. 78.
[202] Ibid., p. 183.
[203] Eising and Kohler-Koch (^{1}2005), p. 16.
[204] Kraft (2006), p. 39.
[205] Eising and Lehringer (^{3}2010), p. 198.
[206] Ibid., p. 199.
[207] Burson Marsteller. (2013). A Guide to Effective Lobbying in Europe. The View of Policy-Makers. http://lobbyingsurvey.burson-marsteller.eu/wp-content/uploads/2013/05/european_lobbying_survey_2013.pdf, visited on June 23, 2013, p. 23; Burson Marsteller describes itself as "a leading global public relations and communications firm' and has itself registered as a professional consulting firm."
[208] Ibid.

Through the allocation of EU grants as part of their programs, the Commission also indirectly funds lobbyists and their entities.[209] Almost all public interest groups are believed to receive the major amount of their budget from such grants.[210] Whereas the allocation of such funding may evoke a certain dependency of interest groups and have an influence on their activities,[211] private consultants and lobbying firms in Brussels have been revealed to even sell their advice to interest groups on how to secure a grant from the Commission in exchange for advice, research, or representation.[212] However, Hix and Høyland consider the Commission as a key institution for "the supply of access to non-state interests."[213] Irrespective of such indirect funding from the Commission, within the EU's political process, lobbying activities are limited to long-term targets.

As Eising and Lehringer note, it is especially the dynamic political agenda of the EU that makes it difficult for interest groups to predict short-term political developments, leaves them often insecure about political options, and forces them to devote considerable resources to monitoring.[214] On average, estimations on the current number of Brussels-based active lobbyists stand between 15,000[215] and 27,000.[216] The EU, in particular, bases its estimates on the assumption that on average every interest-representing entity listed in the TR employs four personnel.[217] Nonetheless, Gentili infers from his research that it is impossible to measure the exact percentage of interest representatives covered by the TR.[218] In 2012, the City of Brussels published an estimation of 25,000 lobbyists. The EU Watchdog Representative is still convinced that this was simply an 'overstatement' used to promote the capital's attractiveness to other lobbyists as their place of business; the City has not clarified the source

---

[209] See Hix and Høyland (^{3}2011), p. 173.
[210] Michalowitz (2007), p. 172.
[211] Eising and Kohler-Koch (^{1}2005), p. 24.
[212] Coen and Richardson (2011), p. 21.
[213] Hix and Høyland (^{3}2011), p. 181.
[214] Eising and Lehringer (^{3}2010), pp. 190f.
[215] Weidenfeld and Wessel (2011), p. 360.
[216] Šefčovič, M. (2013). Speech—Opening Remarks. OECD Forum on Transparency and Integrity in Lobbying of June 27, 2013. http://europa.eu/rapid/press-release_SPEECH-13-581_en.htm?locale=en, visited on July 29, 2013.
[217] Šefčovič (2011), p. 202.
[218] Gentili (2013), p. 14.

of its estimation yet.²¹⁹ Obviously, estimating the *de facto* amount of active lobbyists in Brussels remains an undertaking of impossibility.²²⁰

Considering the question why it is necessary at all to lobby EU institutions, the DLR Employee points to the regular rotation of MEPs and Commissioners due to their five-year terms; neither institution could employ a sufficient pool of experts to cover the huge bandwidth of topics related to the incumbency of these EU officials. As the DLR Employee concludes, without lobbyists many legislative matters would be adopted with deficient consideration of necessary expert knowledge.²²¹ The WWF Employee agrees with this view, adding that whereas politicians tend to discuss issues rather vertically, lobbyists cut across political debates horizontally.²²² Likewise, the MEP also opines that reasonable politics cannot be carried out without solid lobbying: Politicians do not only have to know the views of all actors that might be affected, but also the scope of consequences a legislative action might cause.²²³ The aforementioned views are also reflected by the BM survey: 62 percent of interviewees designated "meeting with industry" as the third most helpful possibility to gather information for decision-making.²²⁴

2.2.5 History of lobbying regulation in the United States

After the right to petition had already been laid down in the Magna Carta²²⁵ of 1215, it was also constituted by the Declaration of Independence of 1776 and incorporated into the constitution of 12 states by then.²²⁶ Kraft marks the hour of birth of US lobbying by the attempt of lobbyists to influence the very first custom law in 1789.²²⁷ The next milestone of lobbying regulation can also be dated back to the 18th century: by the inclusion of *freedom of speech, press, petition, and union* into the first of the 10 amendments of the American Constitution (which were summarized as the 'Bill of Rights') in 1791. This paragraph prevails until today as the constitutional legal legitimation of US lobbying.²²⁸ First attempts to constitute lobbying at Federal level can be dated back to 1876

---

[219] EU Watchdog Representative (2013a).
[220] Nugent (⁷2010), p. 245.
[221] DLR Employee. (2013). Interview of May 27, 2013.
[222] The NGO Representative. (2013). Interview of May 28, 2013.
[223] The MEP. (2013). Interview of May 29, 2013.
[224] BM (2013), p. 18.
[225] Refers to The Great Charter of the Liberties of England.
[226] Clean up Washington. (2005). History of the Lobbying Disclosure Act. http://www.cleanupwashington.org/lobbying/page.cfm?pageid=38#_edn1, visited on April 13, 2013.
[227] Kraft (2006), p. 28.
[228] Kraft (2006), p. 27.

when a resolution of the House of Representatives required lobbyists to register with the House Clerk for the particular congressional session at that time—however, this ruling was not renewed.[229] A number of states even criminalized lobbying by the end of the 19th century.[230]

The first noticeable association of a lobby group in the United States took place after the Civil War (1861–1865) when veterans joined together in the 19th century to push forward their interests.[231] The first official US law on lobbying was the **Foreign Agents Registration Act** (FARA) in 1938,[232] intended to limit the influence and propaganda of foreign agents.[233] Its original purpose was the disclosure of propaganda of Nazi activists.[234] The FARA was altered various times during the 1950s and 1960s: One of the most fundamental amendments was adopted in 1966 when the primary function of FARA shifted from "an antipropagandist tool" to the regulation of grassroots lobbying and lobbying of Congress by foreign agents.[235] However, the overall aim of the act was not the restriction of influence through foreign propaganda, but the identification of such influence as "paid for and distributed by foreign agents."[236]

In 1946, the Congress adopted another key legislation, namely the **Federal Regulation of Lobbying Act** (FRLA).[237] The act was the first comprehensive US law on lobby registration with the CHR and the SOS, and regulated the disclosure of influential attempts directed toward the Congress. Already at that time, lobbyists were required to file quarterly financial reports. Failure to obey this obligation could lead to civil fines of a maximum of $5,000, or one year of

---

[229] Ibid., p. 49.
[230] Clean Up Washington (2005)
[231] Kraft (2006), p. 29.
[232] Ibid., p. 50.
[233] Foreign agents was a term used for any person acting as a lobbyist, public relations representative or attorney for a foreign principal, or any domestic organization subsidized by a foreign principal (foreign government, political party, corporation, entity, or individual organized under the laws of, or having a principal place of business in a foreign nation).
[234] House of Representatives. (1995). Lobbying Disclosure Act of 1995. Report. http://lobbyingdisclosure.house.gov/HReport104-339.pdf, visited on April 23, 2013, p. 6.
[235] Clean Up Washington (2005).
[236] Holman (2008), p. 3.
[237] Straus, J.R. (2013). Lobbying Registration and Disclosure: The Role of the Clerk of the House and the Secretary of the Senate. http://www.fas.org/sgp/crs/misc/RL34377.pdf, visited on April 13, 2013, p. 2.

imprisonment and a three-year prohibition to lobby.[238] In retrospect, the FRLA is criticized for having lacked a code of conduct for lobbying, a supervisory authority, as well as a definition covering all types of lobbyists and allowing for consistent penalties.[239] As a matter of fact, the quantity of interest groups rose after the 1960s. Wilson et al. assume possible factors for this development, such as an increase in economic activities and governmental politics that created new interests and redefined those already existing, or the motivation of individuals to lead such interest groups.[240] As Berry further concludes, the intensified activity of interest representatives not only occurred amid a "period of party decline," but also altered American politics.[241] However, by 1990, only a minor amount of lobbyists complied with the FRLA—therefore, it was "widely perceived as poorly drafted and ineffective."[242]

The act was replaced in 1995 by the **LDA**. By that, lobbyists influencing the Congress were obliged by law to register with the CHR and the SOS, and to regularly report their activities and expenses related to lobbying.[243] Compared to regulations before 1995, the LDA did not only cover obligatory registration for lobbying the Federal Legislative, but also included lobbying activities addressed to Federal administrative agencies.[244] Since the act still incorporated former parts of FRLA and FARA, lobbyists representing foreign governments or foreign political parties had to continue their registration under FARA.[245] As Holman points out, the main intention of the LDA was to serve as a "disclosure regime" to reveal possible corruption between structures of lobbyists, lawmakers, and financial contributors.[246] Generally, the LDA was the final result after a decade-long effort to disclose lobbying in the United States more efficiently.[247]

The **Honest Leadership and Open Government Act** (HLOGA) amended the LDA in 2007. Although the definition of lobbying is now more precise, lobbyists

---

[238] Clean Up Washington (2005); see also Straus, J.R. (2011). Lobbying Registration and Disclosure: Before and After the Enactment of the Honest Leadership and Open Government Act of 2007. http://www.fas.org/sgp/crs/misc/R40245.pdf, visited on April 12, 2013, p. 1.
[239] Wilson et al. (^{12}2011), p. 281; Clean Up Washington (2005); see Holman (2008), p. 2.
[240] Wilson et al. (^{12}2011), pp. 262–264.
[241] Berry (1997), p. 108.
[242] Clean Up Washington (2005).
[243] Wasser (^{3}2007), p. 339; see also the CHR Employee. (2013). Interview of July 3, 2013.
[244] Holman and Luneburg (2012).
[245] Clean Up Washington (2005).
[246] Holman (2008), p. 10.
[247] Clean up Washington (2005)

through HLOGA are obliged to file activity and financial reports more frequently.[248] Generally, the act did not only amend the LDA, but also nonstatutory congressional ethics rules and Federal laws for the financing of campaigns. The HLOGA and subsequent lobbying acts extended the joint responsibility of the CHR and the SOS to implement systems for the registration and reporting of lobbyists.[249] Comparably, the act changed disclosure requirements from semiannual to quarterly reporting on certain contributions and included coalitions and associations into the scope of the LDA.[250] The submission of reports through paper documents was abandoned and filing with the databases of both the SOS and the CHR by a single electronic system was determined.[251] Full electronic filing was required of all lobbyists in 2009.[252] By that, submission became easier to handle and accessibility of documents to the public was simplified.[253] According to Holman, lobbyists in the United States had initially opposed LDA requirements in 1995. However, after its amendments through HLOGA mandatory registration and financial disclosure were "nearly universally accepted as an important pillar of open and honest government in the United States" in 2008.[254] Quite similar to the EU, LDA and HLOGA remain Federal regulations, whereas the single states of the United States maintain their own lobbying regulation.[255]

Through the right to petition, lobbying has directly and indirectly been a traditional basic right of the US citizen; also the development of interest groups is historically conditioned. Due to the fact that legislation in this area has been reviewed and amended various times, it can be identified as a pivotal aspect of US politics. Thus, it is understandable that registration requirements already existed since 1946. With special regard to the inherent concept of political campaigning, the LDA's mandatory scheme is certainly also a mechanism to inhibit corruption possibly resulting from such monetary influence.[256] Equally, the LDA

---

[248] Straus (2011).
[249] Straus (2013), p. 2.
[250] Ibid., p. 5.
[251] Straus (2013), summary.
[252] Straus (2011), p. 8.
[253] Clean Up Washington (2005).
[254] Holman (2008), p. 17.
[255] CHR Employee (2013).
[256] Gentili (2013), p. 10.

can be assessed as a necessary act to replace the "existing patchwork of lobbying disclosure laws with a single, uniform statute,"[257] which in comparison with the FLRA extended the scope of lobbying activities and defined the latter to a more precise degree.[258] By that it strengthened public confidence,[259] and was accepted as an appropriate measure by lobbyists, which is a key precondition for an effective implementation of lobbying disclosure laws.

2.2.6 Lobbying in the United States

Pursuant to Sebaldt, lobbying in the United States is not only **cross-institutional**, but also based on a **pluralistic system of interest procurement**. A structural deficit of US parties as well as a distinct orientation toward the constituencies of Congressmen has led to the development of a **multilevel system** of grassroots lobbying on one side and the Washington lobby on the other. Furthermore, the US lobbying system can be characterized by predominant informal issue networks between lobbyists and political institutions.[260] Whereas Berry argued in 1997 that "Washington law is lobbying law"[261] and that the public perceived interest groups as "cancer, spreading unchecked throughout the politic body, making it gradually weaker, until they eventually kill it."[262] Wilson et al. accentuated that interest groups in the United States are simply inevitable due to the size and diversity of the nation, decentralizing effects of the Constitution and weak political parties.[263] Also in the United States, organized interests try to benefit from coalition building on a short- or long-term basis.[264] According to the scholar Kevin Hula, such coalitions are a key instrument for the aggregation of viewpoints to politics since they 'predigest' policy proposals before passing them to legislators.[265]

---

[257] US Congress, House Committee on the Judiciary. (1995). *Lobbying Disclosure Act of 1995, report to accompany H.R. 2564*, 104th Cong., 1st sess., H.Rept. 104-339. Washington: GPO, p. 2; cited by Straus (2013).

[258] Thunert, M. (^{1}2003). Is that the way we like it? Lobbying in den USA. In: T. Leif and R. Speth (eds.), *Die stille Macht. Lobbyismus in Deutschland*. Wiesbaden: Westdeutscher Verlag, p. 325.

[259] US Congress (1995), p. 2; cited by Straus (2013).

[260] Sebaldt (^{1}2007), p. 105.

[261] Berry (1997), p. 24.

[262] Ibid., p. 19.

[263] Wilson et al. (^{12}2011), p. 261.

[264] Hula, K.W. (1999). *Lobbying Together. Interest Group Coalitions in Legislative Politics*. Washington, DC.: Georgetown University Press, pp. 2, 5.

[265] Ibid., p. 7.

Moreover, the US system creates four powerful institutional incentives for lobbyists. First, the decision-making process is highly fragmented and characterized by a lower degree of party discipline, from which lobbyists could benefit. Second, the system is based on competitive Federalism, since the single states are endowed with a broader political management scope than the German Bundesländer, for instance. As a matter of fact, deputies maintain strong boundaries with their constituencies. Third, lobbyists can therefore attempt to influence the public opinion of constituents by grassroots lobbying. This possibility is complemented by the fourth incentive to benefit from various opportunities of direct democracy at the state level, by which lobbyists can tailor their strategies of approaching politicians.[266] Compared to the EU, US American lobbyists generally apply, to a major degree, tactics of outside lobbying than traditional instruments directly addressed to decision-makers.[267] Due to a huge variety of access possibilities for interest groups to influence nearly any state of the legislative decision procedure, Kraft even speaks of a shared decision-making competence.[268] Beyond that, the aforementioned increase of fragmentation within the pluralistic decision-making system of the United States has also evoked more intensive competition between interest organizations. Sebaldt ascribes this to a growing diversity of interests and thus a growing competition to attract target clientele.[269] According to Woll, it is also a common practice of US lobbyists to try to block political decision by threatening legislators with court action.[270]

Generally, US lobbyists can be categorized by a high degree of professionalism and as a general rule they are often lawyers. The more decisive a particular issue becomes for a certain firm or interest group, the more they tend to disburse lawyers to take judicial action against proposed bills.[271] Interest groups have been an essential part of US politics. Instead of bigger associations or unions, it is especially single-issue groups that have an impact on legislators.[272] In addition to that, hierarchical structures are also regarded to be less distinct

---

[266] Thunert (¹2003), pp. 321f.
[267] Michalowitz (2007), p. 174.
[268] Kraft (2006), p. 48.
[269] Sebaldt (2011), p. 95.
[270] Woll (2005), p. 1.
[271] Woll (2005), p. 5.
[272] Wallace, H. et al. (⁶2010). *Policy-Making in the European Union. The New European Union Series.* Oxford: Oxford University Press, p. 391.

amid US American associations; regional organizations act *de facto* autonomously.²⁷³ According to Wallace et al., instead of concluding compromises, interest groups also favor to polarize. By that, governmental cooperation could become more difficult and gridlock could increase.²⁷⁴

In the United States, lobbying groups can receive funds either from foundation grants, Federal grants, and contracts by which the government does not fund the group directly but single projects of the latter, and finally also through direct mailing to target groups, which is used to promote membership in interest groups and to seek financial support.²⁷⁵ On the other side of the financial bargaining, it is also interest groups that play an important role in election campaigning and funding: Election campaigns in the United States are mainly funded by individual donations or so-called Political Action Committees (PACs).²⁷⁶ Basically, PACs can be formed by any kind of organization and, therefore, also by public interest lobbies.²⁷⁷ Additionally, they do not necessarily have to register themselves as a representative of certain interests. Whereas interest groups and lobbyists do not have permission to distribute directly to such campaigns, they are permitted to take a PAC's lead and to encourage their members to contribute to its funding. Participating in PACs offers a mutual benefit: While candidates receive funding and assistance during the preparation of an election, PAC members gain privileged access to the politician once the incumbency commences.²⁷⁸

Rosenthal distinguishes between five different types of lobbyists in the United States: *Contract Lobbyists* are bound by contract to various clients and operate independently of any organization; *Association Lobbyists* are in-house lobbyists representing business, labor, professionals, and trade associations; *Company Lobbyists* are employed by a single organization to represent a certain business; *Governmental Lobbyists* are employees of associations of local governments; and finally, *Cause Lobbyists* work for a whole range of groups, most of which represent philosophical and ideological interests of the public. This category also includes nonprofit organizations.²⁷⁹ Even if in the United States

---

[273] Sebaldt (2011), p. 102.
[274] Wallace, H. et al (2010⁶), p. 391.
[275] Wilson et al. (¹²2011), pp. 272f.
[276] Friedrich, S. (2010). Measuring Interest Group Activity. CESifo DICE Report 4/2010. http://www.cesifo-group.de/ifoHome/publications/docbase/details.html?docId=14994986, visited on April 21, 2013, p. 38.
[277] Wilson et al. (¹²2011), p. 277.
[278] Michalowitz (2007), pp. 181f.
[279] Rosenthal (1993), p. 22.

every lobbyist is forced by law to register, realistic estimates of the *de facto* amount of lobbyists remain a matter of discussion. Pursuant to Kraft, for instance, the number of lobbyists had increased from around 9,000 in 1955 to an amount between 20,000 and 40,000 in 2004.[280]

2.2.7 Interim conclusion

As the previous chapters divulge, the most lobbied institutions in the EU are the EP and particularly its committees, the European Commission and to a limited degree, the Council of the EU. With regard to the United States, it is likewise the Congress and its committees, the Executive Office of the President, as well as administrative agencies. Whereas EU lobbyists can benefit from a lack of whip and a predominance of national interests, Washington, DC's interest representatives can profit by the habit of members of the Congress to rather stick to the concerns of their constituents than to party discipline. Traditionally, most delegates in the United States are lawyers and businessmen, whereas posts of EU politicians are predominantly held by former public servants.[281] Both political systems are based on a separation of powers[282] and incorporate working parliaments of which the main legislative work is accomplished in committees.[283] Political influence in both capitals is exerted through in-house lobbying, formal and informal organized associations on several levels, as well as by professional public affairs consultancies directed toward several levels.[284] Apart from that, both systems incorporate the concept of 'checks and balances,' even if to the EU citizens this seems less conversant.[285] Nonetheless, governmental bodies in the States act rather independently, whereas the power and control of EU institutions is more intertwined.[286]

As the In-House Lobbyist points out, a key difference between lobbying in the EU and the United States is based on the effect of their activities: Whereas, in the United States it is the overall target of lobbyists to highly curtail the power of a legislative draft or even hinder it from being adopted, this is not possible in Brussels, since most initiatives reach their legislative target once being started. Therefore, in the United States, the legislative process is approached more

---

[280] Kraft (2006), p. 29.
[281] Jäger, W. et al. (^{3}2007). *Regierungssystem der USA. Lehr- und Handbuch*. München: Oldenbourg Wissenschaftsverlag GmbH, pp. 36f.
[282] Hix and Høyland (^{3}2011), p. 54.
[283] Gellner and Kleiber (^{1}2007), p. 42.
[284] Michalowitz (2007), p. 172.
[285] Šefčovič (2011), p. 198.
[286] Michalowitz (2007), p. 179.

judicially and less politically than in the EU.[287] Both approaches also diverge in the fact that lobbying in the United States is proceeded in a more progressive way, which—as compared to the EU—concentrates less on diplomatically establishing networks, which are designed on a long-term basis and built on trust.[288]

Tactics of EU lobbyists are moreover categorized as being more subtle and consensus oriented, compared to more competitive and fragmented strategies applied in Washington, DC.[289] The US interest representatives are also far more likely to employ lobby firms or lawyers for short-term activities and with the target to push forward interests amid a legislative draft procedure—even if this requires investing a large amount of money or court action. Grassroots lobbying is more successful in the United States. Apart from that, both lobbying concepts include instruments of formal and informal consultation. Whereas at either side of the Atlantic, interest groups and lobbyists get directly or indirectly funded by EU or US governmental grants and projects, in the United States, lobbyists can additionally benefit to a high extent from mutual profits of election campaigning they support.[290] As critics argue, US politicians can become reliant on such funding;[291] contrarily, in the EU, the argument is used vice versa when scientists warn that interest groups could become increasingly dependent on Commission funding. Holman and Luneburg point furthermore to another basic difference: The promotion of transparency is only one motivation for North American lobbying regulation besides a decrease in political corruption and an enhanced accountability of executives. On the contrary, transparency is the "driving force behind most of today's regulatory campaigns in Europe."[292]

With regard to the legislative basis of lobbying registration, a survey by Craig Holman about the attitude of US and EU lobbyists (2008) revealed that 8.1 percent support no type of public registration at all, 25.7 percent back a voluntary register, and 66.2 percent favor a mandatory one. Interestingly, breaking down the results revealed that nearly all US interest representatives enhance

---

[287] In-House Lobbyist (2013).
[288] Woll (2005), p. 14.
[289] Ibid., p. 9.
[290] Ibid., p. 4
[291] McFarland, A. (^{1}2010). Interest Group Theory. In: L. Maisel et al. (eds.), *The Oxford Handbook of American Political Parties and Interest Groups*. New York: Oxford University Press Inc., p. 50.
[292] Holman and Luneburg (2012).

obligatory registry compared with Brussels respondents, of which only a slight majority supports this approach.[293]

2.3 Regulation and registration

Lobbying regulation alludes to the intervention of lobbyists' addressees by formal means. Regulatory measures are designed to develop structures, procedures, and principles to administer interaction of addressees and actors, to limit negative consequences of lobbying and create and foster the capacity of political work.[294] In addition, the special form of lobbying regulation allows citizens and practitioners to gain insight into influence, which is exerted within the policy process.[295] Markus Krajewski defines three types of lobbying regulation: namely, professional regulation, such as associations implementing their own code of conduct; institutional registers; and "mandatory legislation or other legally binding standards."[296] Lobbying regulation can differ according to its object of regulation, type of regulator, level of decision-making process, and level of regulation, such as macro, meso or micro, as well as the supranational or national level.[297] According to Kraft, an efficient system of lobbying regulation needs to contain the following components: a clear definition of lobbyists and their activities; a scope that covers any form of lobbying; the possibility to punish nonobedience; and finally a liable authority of enforcement.[298] Nations other than the EU Members that have already adopted such mechanisms are the United States (1946), Canada (1989), Taiwan (2008), Australia (2008), and Israel (2008), for instance.[299]

A common instrument of lobbying regulation is a lobby register: Such a register, in particular, can be defined as a list of individuals, organizations, or institutions

---

[293] Holman, C. (2009). Lobbying Reform in the United States and the European Union: Progress on Two Continents. In: C. McGrath (ed.), *Interest Groups and Lobbying in the United States, and Comparative Perspectives*. Lewiston, ME: Edwin Mellen Press. http://www.centreurope-montreal.ca/fileadmin/confluence/2949195/paper_cholman_20 090525.pdf, visited on May 22, 2013; cited by Holman and Luneburg (2012).
[294] Ahrens (¹2007), p. 124.
[295] *Journals of the Research Group on Socialism and Democracy* online. (2012). Lobbying in the European Commission: Open or Secret? http://sdonline.org/56/volume-25-no-2/lobbying-the-european-commission-open-or-secret1/, visited on March 29, 2013.
[296] Krajewskis, M. (2013a). *Legal Study. Legal Framework for a Mandatory EU Lobby Register and Regulations*. Erlangen-Nürnberg: University of Erlangen-Nürnberg, p. 4.
[297] Ahrens (¹2007), p. 140.
[298] Kraft (2006), pp. 64f.
[299] Years in brackets refer to the time of first implementation; *Journals of the Research Group on Socialism and Democracy* online (2012).

that are involved in a certain activity of which the register intends to provide an overview. In detail, a lobbying register can be designed to disclose information about lobbyists' names and contacts, fields of activity and interest, followed legislative dossiers, members and staff involved, as well as targets. According to the EU, its TR in particular is purposed to function both as a "reference directory" and a "search tool."[300] In addition, a TR can also be regarded as an instrument to *monitor*[301] lobbyism, since its public accessibility also invites organizations, journalists, academics, or citizens to use the register's data for gaining an overview about the lobbying process and its actors. The possibility of being publicly listed in such a register is also perceived as a "matter of good reputation."[302] As the *Journal of the Research Group on Socialism and Democracy* argues, citizens are keen on knowing those who influence policy, on being informed about political outcomes, and on how the latter might affect their lives. Therefore, a "robust system of registration could enlighten and empower them."[303]

2.4 Transparency

Transparency from a political angle can be defined as the obviousness and understandability of political and administrative proceedings and decisions.[304] It can create a political instrument for citizens to intervene as soon as political outcomes are considered dissatisfactory, and thus to encourage them in realizing their political will. Therefore, it makes political development less opaque through vista and can furthermore establish trust toward political institutions.[305] By that, it affects the behavior of the political elite, citizen attitudes, and the exercise of democratic control directed toward these elites.[306] Beyond that, it can be applied to increase the public legitimacy of a political system.[307] Whereas Leif and Speth, with respect to lobbying, deem transparency as an

---

[300] JTRS (2012b), p. 5.
[301] Woll (2005), p. 8.
[302] Commission Representative (2013a).
[303] *Journals of the Research Group on Socialism and Democracy* online (2012).
[304] Rittershofer, C. (2007). *Lexikon Politik, Staat, Gesellschaft. 3600 aktuelle Begriffe von Abberufung bis Zwölfmeilenzone.* München: dtv, p. 674.
[305] Hart, T. (2011). Mehr Transparenz für die stillen Mächtigen. In: Leif and SPETH, R. (eds.), (¹2003). *Die stille Macht. Lobbyismus in Deutschland.* Wiesbaden: Westdeutscher Verlag, p. 63
[306] Moser, C. (2001). *How Open is 'Open as Possible'? Three Different Approaches to Transparency and Openness in Regulating Access to EU Documents.* Political Science Series No. 80. Vienna: Institute for Advanced Studies, p. 4.
[307] See ibid., p. 3.

essential instrument,[308] Holman and Luneburg even ascribe to it the power of preventing executives from corruption and to level the playing field.[309] Today, transparency is not only a key factor of good administration[310] in the policy of an open dialogue, but together with trust it lies "at the heart of good decision making and good lobbying."[311] However, definitions of transparency vary due to its numerous approaches and according to the structures for which it can be applied.[312] Perceiving policy-making from a bargaining perspective, some scholars even argue that too much openness may jeopardize negotiations and might even cause attitudes such as aversion. Therefore, information in a transparent sense should be held back if necessary and be revealed only where it is appropriate.[313]

From a legal point of view, transparency as related to the political work of the EU is particularly manifested by Article 11(1) and (2) Treaty on EU (TEU), ruling that

> the institutions shall, by appropriate means, give citizens and representative associations the opportunity to make known and publicly exchange their views in all areas of Union action

as well as that

> The institutions shall maintain an open, transparent and regular dialogue with representative associations and civil society.

By that, the EU does not only guarantee interest representatives the right to conduct their work and express their opinion on a certain legislative issue vis-à-vis the institutions, but to a certain degree also creates a general basis for the TR as a means to support such an open and transparent dialogue. Article 11(2) TEU is furthermore fortified by Article 15(1) Treaty on the Functioning of the EU (TFEU), stating that

> In order to promote good governance and ensure the participation of civil society, the Union institutions, bodies, offices and agencies shall conduct their work as openly as possible.

Furthermore, Article 15(3) TFEU even determines that institutions, bodies, offices, and agencies shall ensure proceedings to be 'transparent.'

---

[308] Leif and Speth ([1]2003), p. 28.
[309] Holman and Luneburg (2012).
[310] Moser (2011), p. 2.
[311] Europa (2011d).
[312] Moser (2011), p. 2.
[313] Moser (2011), p. 5.

3 Comparison of lobbying registration in the EU and the United States

3.1 The European Union

3.1.1 Implementation of the Transparency Register

The EU defines the TR as a "voluntary scheme, supported by a public interactive tool [...] to add transparency to the EU decision-making process."[314] Data collected by the TR seek to inform about organizations and self-employed individuals that engage in activities "with the objective of influencing the decision-making processes of the European Union." The TR is designed as a 'one-stop shop' service to be applied by EU public officials and personnel, EU interest representatives, as well as by the EU's citizens.[315] Its framework includes a code of conduct, a set of guidelines, as well as a complaint mechanism.[316] Registration and consultation of the register are free of charge and processed via a web interface. Therefore, all submitted data will be publicly available apart from the information about contact persons of registered entities, which are used for internal purposes only.[317] According to the IIA, data have to be renewed annually, unless a quality check by the JTRS leads to an additional request for an update.[318]

As emphasized in the annual report of the JTRS, the TR ranks among those registration systems that provide the "widest range of information" and can be applied to "the widest playing field." Registration with the TR is a precondition of the EP "for facilitated access to its buildings"[319] through the distribution of access passes. However, the IIA rules that "registration shall not confer an automatic entitlement" for the reception of such a pass.[320] EP accreditation can only be requested online; each individual applicant has to prove identity and its affiliation with the registered entity to the Parliament's Accreditation Office

---

[314] JTRS (2012b), p. 4.
[315] Ibid., 1.1.
[316] European Parliament. (2013a). Rules of Procedure. http://www.europarl.europa.eu/sides/getDoc.do?pubRef=-//EP//NONSGML+RULES-EP+20130204+0+DOC+PDF+V0//EN&language=EN, visited on May 1, 2013, pp. 176f.
[317] Europa. (2011a). Q's & A's: Transparency Register. http://europa.eu/rapid/press-release_MEMO-11-446_en.htm?locale=en, visited on May 1, 2013.
[318] JTRS Staff. (2013a). Interview of May 15, 2013.
[319] JTRS (2012b), p. 15, 3.3.
[320] Official Journal of the European Union (2011), Art. 22.

(EP's Security). Security responds within a maximum of three days' time to approve or reject accreditation. Access can be granted for six months or a whole year, but cards need to be activated at a special TR reception desk for every EP visit.[321]

Access passes contain the holder's photograph, surname, forename, as well as their employer's, and should be worn visibly anytime within parliamentary premises to distinguish their owners from other visitors. As a matter of principle, the attendance of EP meetings is limited to those open to the public.[322] After numerous organizations requested to eliminate limits of the maximum amount of cardholders per registrant, limitations were abolished. Nevertheless, no more than four individuals of one single registered entity are allowed to sojourn in the Parliament's premises at once.[323] The delivery of access cards is not the only advantage interest representatives can gain: As part of their registration they are expected to tick policy areas of their particular legislative concern. With regard to their individual choice, the European Commission offers to inform them about the launch of public consultations or roadmaps via an e-mail alerting service.[324] Registration is furthermore promoted by such consultations: Once results are published, the Commission publicly distinguishes between contributions from TR registrants and external entities by listing them separately. Apart from that, the institution explicitly encourages nonregistrants to join.[325]

◯ **Who is expected to register?**

Irrespective of their legal status, any organization and self-employed individual engaged in activities within the scope of the register is generally required to register with the TR.[326] However, governments of EU Member States or third countries as well as international intergovernmental organizations and their diplomatic missions do not fall under this scope. Churches are excluded from the expectation to register, although their representative offices, legal bodies, and associations should disclose their information in the TR. Also political parties are not considered to fall under the scope of registrants, even if this is not

---

[321] JTRS Staff (2013a).
[322] European Parliament (2013a), p. 175.
[323] JTRS Staff. (2013d). E-mail received on June 4, 2013.
[324] Europa (2011a).
[325] Commission Representative (2013a).
[326] JTRS. (2012c). Transparency Register. Frequently Asked Questions. http://ec.europa.eu/transparencyregister/info/your-organisation/faq.do?locale=en, visited on January 16, 2014, p. 3.

valid for any organization that they support or create and that exert activities related to the TR. Finally, also local, regional, and municipal authorities are not expected to disclose their data, whereas any office, legal body, network, or association representing them is clearly concerned by the register, as soon as exerting a certain influence vis-à-vis EU institutions.[327] Registration is not limited by location—thus, registrants do not necessarily have to be based in Brussels if their activities still form part of the register's scope. Considering membership, turnover, or employees, a minimum threshold for registration does not exist.[328] With respect to the plurality of actors, registrants are subdivided into the following six sections:[329] (I) professional consultancies/law firms/self-employed consultants; (II) in-house lobbyists and trade/professional associations; (III) NGOs; (IV) think tanks, research and academic institutions; (V) organizations representing churches and religious communities; and (VI) organizations representing local, regional, and municipal authorities, other public or mixed entities, etc.[330]

○ **Which activities are concerned by the scope of the TR?**
Generally, the register embraces all activities covered by Article 11 TFEU.[331] In detail, "all activities [...] carried out with the objective of directly or indirectly influencing the formulation or implementation of policy and the decision-making processes of the EU institutions" need to be disclosed. The IIA lists certain channels or media for exerting such influence, therefore, means of communication can involve outsourcing, media, contracts with professional intermediaries, think tanks, platforms, forums, campaigns, and grassroots initiatives. Moreover, the IIA defines lobbying activities as "contacting members, officials or other staff of the EU institutions, preparing, circulating and communicating letters, information material or discussion papers and position papers." Also the organization of general or social events, meetings, promotional activities or

---

[327] Transparency Register. (2013a). Who is Expected to Register? http://ec.europa.eu/transparencyregister/info/your-organisation/whoRegister.do?locale=en, visited on January 17, 2014.
[328] Europa (2011a).
[329] JTRS (2012b), 1.1.
[330] Official Journal of the European Union (2011), Annex I.
[331] Article 11(1) TEU: The institutions shall, by appropriate means, give citizens and representative associations the opportunity to make known and publically exchange their views in all areas of Union action; (2) The institutions shall maintain an open, transparent and regular dialogue with representative associations and civil society; (3) The EC shall carry out broad consultations with parties concerned in order to ensure that the unions actions are coherent and transparent; Europa (2011a).

conferences, as well as inviting Members, officials, or other personnel of EU institutions are identified as such activities.[332] Action excluded from registration are the provision of legal and professional advice during trial, such as that given by law firms; operations of social partners which form part of the 'social dialogue,' such as that by trade unions; and direct responses to an EU request.[333]

⊃ **Which information is expected to be disclosed?**

Information submitted to the TR needs to contain the registrant's name, address, phone number, e-mail address, and website. Contact details must further include the person legally responsible for the registering entity, as well as the "permanent person in charge of EU relations." Registry needs to contain the number of persons employed for relevant activities, whereas cardholders will be listed by name as well once their application for accreditation is accepted. Further information should be provided about goals and remits; fields of interest; activities; countries in which the entity actively operates; affiliations to networks, such as associations; and if applicable, the number of members.[334] Referring to the latest financial year closed, financial figures should cover a whole year of activity and be annually updated, even if a specific deadline by a certain day does not exist. Professional consultancies, law firms, and self-employed consultants (section I) need to disclose details on their turnover as well as "the relative weight attaching to their clients." Details are required to be submitted in bracket sizes of €50,000 (for €0–499,000), €100,000 (€500,000–1,000,000), and €250,000 (for sums exceeding €1,000,000). Since the financial declaration of section I registrants does not eliminate their clients' obligation to declare their own contractual activities in their registries, double-counting is not excluded. In-house lobbyists as well as trade and professional associations (section II) are required to base their estimation on their expenses related to activities covered by the TR, whereas registrants of the sections III–VI additionally have to list their overall budget including a "breakdown of the main sources of funding." In addition, all registrants are expected to disclose the amount and source of EU funding of the most recent financial year

---

[332] Official Journal of the European Union (2011), IV. (8).
[333] JTRS (2012c), p. 3.
[334] Official Journal of the European Union (2011), Annex II.

closed.[335] Zero-Euro declarations are permitted, but require an appropriate justification by the registrant.[336]

According to the guidelines of the JTRS, cost estimates for activities under the register's scope should be based on the following five components: (1) staff costs calculated on the basis of staff time dedicated to lobbying activities; (2) administrative costs; (3) "outsourced activity costs, consulting fees and subcontracted activities"; (4) operational expenditure, such as for media use or campaigning; and (5) membership fees, contribution, and participation costs.[337] However, due to the obvious different treatment of sections with regard to their particular requirements for financial disclosure, Gentili speaks of a "disparity of treatment" that prevented to "level the playing field for registrants."[338]

The voluntary approach of the TR and its rather broad definitions in particular often cause criticism among scholars and politicians. However, it is especially the voluntary conception that covers a very broad scope of organizations and thus can theoretically increase the level of disclosure. In addition, the six subsections of registrants allow for a better overview and indicate at first sight the general interest of the particular entity. Moreover, to maximize attractiveness of a voluntary register, registrants are granted certain privileges from which they can obviously benefit. Even if the TR was officially designed as a 'one-stop-shop,' relevant data about its *de facto* target group for application are nonexistent, and the application especially by EP staff simply cannot be taken for granted.

3.1.2 Legal basis

The Treaties of the EU lack an explicit EU competence for the adoption of binding law regulating lobbying activities.[339] However, Commissioner Šefčovič underlined in 2011 that the TR's review process might allow for the possibility to implement a mandatory register.[340] In 2009, the EP called for "an interinstitutional agreement between the Council, the Commission and Parliament on a

---

[335] Ibid.
[336] JTRS. (2012a). Transparency Register Compliance Guidelines, Edition No. 3. http://europa.eu/transparencyregister/info/your-organisation/guidanceFinancial.do?locale=en, visited on January 17, 2014, p. 3.
[337] JTRS (2012a), pp. 3f.
[338] Gentili (2013), p. IV.
[339] Krajewski (2013a), p. 7.
[340] Europa (2011c), p. 25.

common mandatory register"[341] including a common code of ethical conduct.[342] According to the Commission Representative, a change of the TR's constitution is not a question of exigency, but a legal one: Even if the EP declared in 2008 that it was "aware of the legal basis for a mandatory register provided by the Treaty of Lisbon,"[343] the Commission is still not convinced that the Treaties *de facto* provide a basis for a mandatory register—at least not in the sense to oblige public affairs professionals to register for exercising their profession. Furthermore, such an obligation might be considered as restriction of their freedom of enterprise.[344] Given the fact that 28 Member States would have to agree on a necessary legislative compromise, the Commission Representative does not deem a change of Treaties realistic.[345] The MEP is concerned about the feasibility to draw a dividing line through legislation: With certain contact intensity, even a private person could be called a lobbyist, such as a farmer complaining to MEPs in Brussels about the low level of milk prices.[346] However, Krajewski, as the author of the first official scientific study about a "legal framework for a mandatory EU lobby register and regulations," argues that asking a certain profession to register is the "lowest level of regulatory interference."[347]

As a matter of principle, the European Commission needs to justify every legislative proposal by a legislative basis. Without such a basis, the EU is only authorized to conclude political programs, incentive measures, initiatives, or interinstitutional agreements among others. However, they do not have any legislative character. Even if Article 15 TFEU determines that

> In order to promote good governance and ensure the participation of civil society, the Union institutions, bodies, offices and agencies shall conduct their work as openly as possible,

the Treaty does not authorize the adoption of legislation here. Article 50(1) TFEU constitutes that "in order to attain freedom of establishment as regards

---

[341] Official Journal of the European Union. (2009). 12.11.2009. 2009/C 271 E/06, 11, p. 50.
[342] Ibid., 16, p. 50.
[343] European Parliament. (2008). European Parliament resolution of May 8, 2008 on the development of the framework for the activities of interest representatives (lobbyists) in the European institutions (2007/2115(INI)). http://www.europarl.europa.eu/sides/get Doc.do?pubRef=-//EP//TEXT+TA+P6-TA-2008-0197+0+DOC+XML+V0//EN, visited on June 12, 2013, p. 16.
[344] Commission Representative (2013a).
[345] Ibid.
[346] The MEP (2013).
[347] Krajewski, M. (2013b). Comment raised during live debate "Mandatory or Voluntary? Time for a Register that Really Works!", European Parliament. June 17, 2013.

a **particular activity**"; the EP and the Council shall conclude directives through the ordinary legislative procedure. However, the EU would have to clarify whether lobbying can be classified as a particular activity. Another restriction might be laid down in Article 50(2)(c) TFEU which rules that the EP, the Commission, and the Council should abolish

> administrative procedures and practices, whether resulting from national legislation or from agreements previously concluded between Member States
>
> that could be
>
> an **obstacle to freedom of establishment**.

Therefore, it needs to be judicially proved that a mandatory register itself does not constitute such an obstacle. This is underlined by Article 50(2)(f) determining that the EU should affect "the progressive **abolition of restrictions** on freedom of establishment in every branch of activity" including the establishment of agencies, branches, or subsidiaries in a Member State's territory. According to Article 59(1) TFEU, by the ordinary legislative procedure the EP and the Council shall enact directives "to achieve the **liberalization of a specific service**." Further clarification needs to determine whether lobbying can be identified as a specific service and can, therefore, be argued to require liberalization. However, if this was the case, this article might rather be referred to as an argument against a mandatory register. Furthermore, Article 352 TFEU lays down that

> If action by the Union should prove **necessary**, within the framework of the policies defined in the Treaties, to attain one of the **objectives** set out in the Treaties, and the Treaties have not provided the necessary powers, the Council [...] shall adopt [.] appropriate measures.

In this context, the EU would have to justify why the establishment of a mandatory register is necessary and demands appropriate measures, and to what extent a compulsory TR would constitute an objective of the Treaties. According to the GSC Representative, some participants in the discussion suggest basing a legally binding register on a combination of Article 352 TFEU with Article 11(1) and (2) TEU,[348] stipulating that the institutions *shall, by appropriate means, give citizens and representative associations the opportunity to make known and publicly exchange their views in all areas of Union action* and shall maintain a regular dialogue with such associations and the civil society that is

---

[348] GSC Representative (2013).

open and transparent. However, the application of Article 352 TFEU requires Council unanimity and the consent of the EP.

Despite the fact that the discussion about mandatory lobbying registration in the EU had started decades ago, the first "published thorough academic analysis" was launched only in June 2013 by Markus Krajewski from the Erlangen-Nürnberg University.[349] The study's author defines it as a key aspect that the TR should be binding on institutions, their staff, and lobbyists, but points out that the IIA cannot constitute for the same formal binding obligation as mandatory legislation does.[350] Therefore, he explains that a legal basis can indeed be found in Article 298(1) TFEU by the ruling that *In carrying out their missions, the institutions, bodies, offices and agencies of the Union shall have the support of an open, efficient and independent European administration.* Further pursuant to Article 298(2), the EP and the Council "acting by means of regulations in accordance with the ordinary legislative procedure, shall establish provisions to that end." As argued, this Article could be applied for lobbyists that address "EU institutions engaged in administrative tasks."[351] However, activities under the scope of this Article are limited to administrative staff and services of the EP and the Commission, and exclude Members of both institutions serving as legislators.[352] Therefore, the aforementioned Article should be applied alongside the **doctrine of implied powers**: Developed by the ECJ, it determines EU institutions to take legislative action even if a legal basis is not laid down in the Treaties. By that, the competence laid down in Article 298(1) and (2) could be complemented by the inclusion of legislative activities.[353] As Krajewski adds, a regulation based on a combination of both could be passed by the OLP[354] and needs to be adopted in the form of a binding EU regulation.[355] According to the MEP, debating the legal possibility to implement a mandatory EU register is one of the key issues during the revision procedure of the TR.[356] In case a legal basis is found, amendments require an agreement of Commissioner Šefčovič and the MEP. Furthermore, both the College of Commissioners

---

[349] Krajewski (2013b).
[350] Krajewski (2013a), p. 6
[351] Article (1): In carrying out their missions, the institutions, bodies, offices and agencies of the Union shall have the support of an open, efficient and independent European administration.
[352] Krajewski (2013a), p. 9.
[353] Ibid., p. 10.
[354] Ibid., p. 3.
[355] Ibid., p. 7.
[356] The MEP (2013).

and the parliamentary Conference of Presidents have to agree. Major changes about the IIA have to be voted in the Parliament's plenary, once the Committee of the European Parliament on Constitutional Affairs has approved them.[357]

The most common argument against a mandatory constitution of the TR is its lacking legal basis. Despite the fact that several articles could theoretically be applied for the purpose of redefining the EU's lobbying regulation, they seemingly were not regarded as legislatively sufficient in the past or a mandatory register was simply not intended by a political majority. Even if suggestions of the recently published study by Krajewski might indeed be a step closer to constituting a legal basis for a mandatory TR, this would require an official confirmation by the EU. Additionally, a combination of Article 298 with the implied powers doctrine would further require the agreement of all 28 Member States, which cannot be guaranteed.

3.1.3 Instruments of control and penalties

The JTRS is in charge of the TR's management, supervision, and awareness raising. These activities further embrace the implementation of a three-step system of quality control through **random quality checks, complaints, and alerts**.[358] To handle quality checks, an IT-generated random list of registrants is produced, which the JTRS applies to contrast the information filed with publicly accessible information. In the event that quality checks divulge inaccuracies, registrants are granted 10 working days for response before their entry is temporarily suspended from the TR, and another four weeks before disbarment.[359] According to the annual report of the JTRS, 404 quality checks (a weekly average of 15) were undertaken between March and September 2012. However, it is worth noting that checks on alerts are included into this count.[360] Alerts can be raised to the Secretariat by anyone.[361] In comparison to complaints, which were implemented as a rather formal instrument, alerts are described as a 'lighter' everyday tool allowing for faster reactions to inadequate information. Furthermore, alerts are the more common form of complaints, which the JTRS receives.[362]

---

[357] JTRS Staff (2013a).
[358] JTRS (2012b), 1.2.1, 1.3.2.3; see also: Official Journal of the European Union (2011), 21.
[359] JTRS Staff (2013a).
[360] JTRS (2012b), 1.3.2.1.
[361] Šefčovič (2011), p. 201.
[362] JTRS (2012b), 1.3.2.3.

As the third monitoring tool, an individual or an organization can raise official complaints if they identify a possible breach of the TR's code of conduct in the entry of a registrant.[363] As a next step, the registrant concerned has to submit an update of data as well as an explanation within 10 working days. The failure to do so leads to temporary suspension from the TR for a period of eight weeks, including 10 working days for reaction. During suspension, entries are no longer publicly accessible, but can be edited by their registrants. Eight weeks in total are granted for an update of information and the submission of an explanation before the entry is disbarred.[364] From March to September 2012, the JTRS examined five formal complaints, all of which were unintentional breaches of the code of conduct.[365] Table 3 below gives an overview about the amount of checks conducted and the number of checks that revealed noncompliance with the code of conduct.

Table 3. JTRS366 checks on TR registrants

March-September 2012	Total	Compliant	Non-compliant
Random checks	289	172	117
Checks on alerts	115	17	98
Total checks	404	189	215

As the table reveals, more than half of the registries checked (53 percent) proved to be inaccurate. This result should be deemed insufficient and lead to measures that could avoid such a high degree of inaccuracies in the future. For the execution of quality checks, the JTRS measures the quality of data against its general criterion that information needs to be "comprehensible and realistic for the citizen."[367] The Secretariat is bound by the IIA to regularly publish guidelines about how requirements for registration are fulfilled best. If considering the TR's various types of entities to be registered, according to the JTRS Staff it is pivotal to "provide a certain level of flexibility" as to allow those defined entities to include the broadest possible scope of groups. However, it remains difficult for the JTRS to provide detailed instructions that can equally be applied

---

[363] Ibid., 1.3.2.2.
[364] Ibid., 1.3.2.1.
[365] Ibid., 1.3.2.2.
[366] JTRS (2012b), 1.3.2.1.
[367] JTRS Staff (2013a).

by all. Moreover, this flexibility prevents information from being entirely "comparable yet."[368] Apart from that, the BM Consultant suggests to bear in mind the administrative effort that would be requisite if the Secretariat intended to control all financial statements for accuracy.[369] As previous quality checks indicated, some filing mistakes are common. Therefore, the JTRS started approaching this category of checks with the more systematic approach to regroup entities whose filing mistakes are similar. Some of the most common faults are submitting zero euros as financial estimates for lobbying-related activities or entering zero personnel for the amount of staff employed for such duties.[370]

For breaches of the code of conduct, the institutions have designed a four-step system of measures: (1) In case noncompliance is unintended and immediately corrected, the entity concerned receives a written notification that points out the facts of a breach and asks for correction. The matter is not publicly notified in the TR, access passes are not withdrawn. (2) If noncompliance proves to be deliberate and the registrant is identified to necessitate a change of behavior or "rectification of information in the register," the individual or organization can be temporarily suspended for a period of up to six months or until inaccuracies are corrected. For the duration of the suspension, the measure will be publicly notified in the entry of the registrant concerned, while accredited individuals can keep their badges. (3) Persistent noncompliance with the TR's code in the form of an unchanged behavior or failure to correct inaccurate data within the deadline given leads to a removal of the entity from the TR for one year. Additionally, the JTRS will publicly notify the measure in its registry and withdraw access passes. (4) Finally, the consequence for "serious, deliberate non-compliance" is a removal for two years as well as a public notification and the withdrawal of access cards.[371] As of May 23, 2013, 3,655 registrants have been disbarred by the JTRS for "various reasons," such as failure to provide an annual update or to respond to a quality check.[372] If the registrant begins the essential steps after a temporary suspension, registries can be reactivated by the

---

[368] Ibid.
[369] The BM Consultant. (2013). Interview of July 3, 2013.
[370] JTRS Staff (2013a).
[371] European Parliament. (2011). Interinstitutional agreement on a common TR between the Parliament and the Commission. EP decision of May 11, 2011 on conclusion of an interinstitutional agreement between the EP and the Commission on a common TR. http://www.europarl.europa.eu/pdf/lobbyists/2011/P7_TA-PROV(2011)0222_EN.pdf, visited on June 15, 2013, Annex IV.
[372] JTRS Staff (2013a).

JTRS. If the individual or entity concerned was disbarred from the TR, its data will entirely be removed and the entity will have to register anew.[373]

Due to the IIA's nonlegal character and rather limited personnel resources of the JTRS, scrutiny is to a certain degree intended to remain a responsibility of the public, especially through complaints and alerts. While this can certainly be regarded as a modern involvement of citizens in democratic system of governance, the accuracy of all entries can generally not be guaranteed. The four-step mechanism imposes measures for noncompliance depending on the gravity of the breach of code and thus allows for individual consequences. Moreover, such measures as public notifications and temporal or permanent removal from the register can be identified as the attempt to enhance compliance by registrants through penalties of rather reputational nature. What might be debatable here is the fact that during any temporary suspension period, cardholders of the entity concerned are still allowed to enter parliamentary premises—according to the IIA, passes do not have to be withdrawn, unless the registrant is permanently disbarred from the TR.[374]

3.1.4 Effectiveness and criticism

A certain extent of TR registrants was transferred from the ROIR's previous amount of approximately 4,000 entities during the TR's first year of operation. As of July 15, 2013, the TR's overall number of registries has increased to 5,844. Still, in-house lobbyists and trade/professional associations form the largest group of registrants with a share of 49.9 percent, whereas 26.1 percent are NGOs, 11.6 percent represent consultancies and law firms, and 7.2 percent belong to the category of think tanks and academic institutions. Local, regional, and municipal authorities are represented by 4.6 percent and finally 0.56 percent are categorized as organizations representing churches and religious communities. Figure 1 below shows the development of registrants within the period from the TR's launch till July 2013.

---

[373] JTRS Staff (2013c).
[374] JTRS (2012b), 1.3.2.1.

Figure 1. Transparency register—weekly evolution of registrants[375]

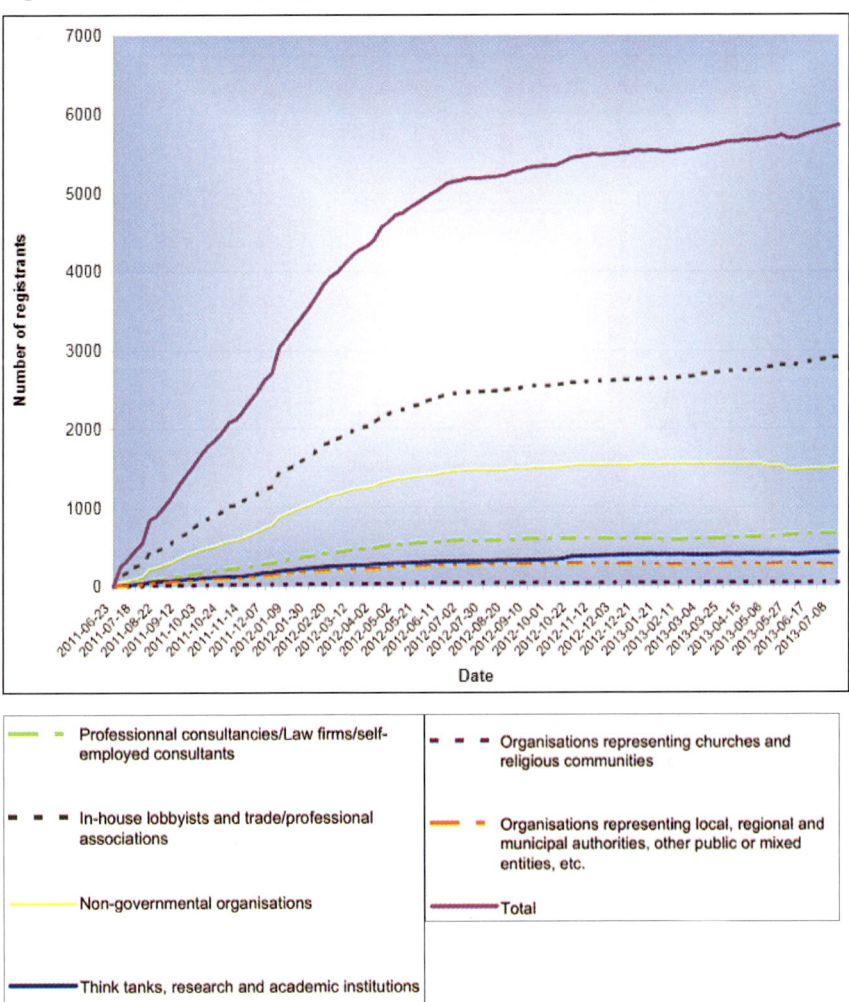

Despite the watchdog's conclusion that the general number of TR entries "boosted" in the past, ALTER-EU hesitates to refer to these figures as the "right

---

[375] JTRS. (2013). Transparency Register Statistics. http://ec.europa.eu/transparency/docs/reg/new_statistiques_en.pdf, visited on July 29, 2013.

indicator for judging" the register's effectiveness.[376] Key criticism by the organizations focuses on outdated information, undisclosed or incomplete client lists, and financial over- or underreporting.[377] Furthermore, the organization assails that registrants listing the highest level of spending are rather small or politically less significant. The TR does not reflect realistic lobbying expenditures in the EU and, thus, provides a misleading picture of "big players" in EU lobbying.[378] However, this assumption might be a fallacy, as the In-House Lobbyist points out: A higher amount of personnel and financial resources for lobbying activities cannot automatically be equated with lobbying of higher quality. Conversely, the employment of highly efficient lobbyists might require fewer personnel in general and could thus reduce the overall budget for lobbying resources.[379]

As still argued by ALTER-EU, the TR is "clearly not de facto mandatory" since more than 100 large companies as well as numerous consultancies, lobby groups, and MEP-industry forums are missing from the register,[380] such as Amazon or Goldman Sachs.[381] In addition, research revealed that 11 among the 50 largest European enterprises (22 percent) are not registered in the TR yet.[382] However, it needs to be kept in mind that some imputations of ALTER-EU proved to be simply untrue in the past: Beyond that, some entities criticized by the ALTER-EU report of 2012 for avoiding registration, filed registries in 2013, for instance such 'big players' as ThyssenKrupp, Metro, Monsato, and the Deutsche Bank.[383] Irrespectively, the Commission considers the current amount of 5,844 registrants a sufficient result,[384] while Commissioner Šefčovič in addition describes the TR as an important source of information for the public as well as the EU to gain an overview about interest representatives.[385] In fact,

---

[376] ALTER-EU. (2013). Rescue the Register! How to Make EU Lobby Transparency Credible and Reliable. http://www.alter-eu.org/sites/default/files/documents/Rescue_the_Register_report_25June2013.pdf, visited on July 29, 2013, p. 9.
[377] Ibid., p. 11.
[378] Ibid., pp. 12f.
[379] In-House Lobbyist (2013).
[380] ALTER-EU (2013), p. 3; Conversely to the watchdog's report which argues that these forums are officially recognized by the EP, they are de facto not considered as official parliamentary bodies.
[381] De Clerck, P. (2013). Comment raised during live debate "Mandatory or Voluntary? Time for a Register That Really Works!" European Parliament. June 17, 2013.
[382] See Handelsblatt (2013). Die 500 größten Unternehmen Europas. No. 110, 12.06.2013, Seite 1, 4-7.
[383] See Transparency Register of the European Union.
[384] Commission Representative (2013a).
[385] Šefčovič (2011), p. 200.

the website of the TR was visited by an average of 7,000 unique visitors per month in 2012.[386]

Results of a TR-focused public consultation of 2012 divulged that 70 percent among registrants were confronted with difficulties to provide the information requested. Most problems arose in the context of providing the concise number of staff involved (as for 20.5 percent) and financial disclosure (20 percent).[387] Inconveniences were to a certain degree also experienced by the interviewees: As the WWF Employee explained, in the beginning the World Wild Fund for Nature (WWF) was confronted with some difficulties to figure out how to clearly define its quantity of staff employed for tasks under the TR's scope. Calculating its relevant budget was a 'hit and miss' at the start, but was improved and done more regularly over the years. In total, registration took three to four days.[388] As the BUSINESSEUROPE Employee explains, the organization probably spent "a few hundred hours" for registering to guarantee that it considered as much information as available to provide "precise, correct and justifiable data."[389] As the DLR Employee furthermore notes, financial updates cannot be completed before the year-end financial statement of an entity is available.[390] For matters of a more efficient controlling, ALTER-EU suggests that the JTRS should examine registries for inaccuracies immediately after their submission. Even though the JTRS would embrace the possibility to do so,[391] especially with regard to its resources this recommendation seems simply too difficult to realize. The BDI Employee opposes this proposition, stating that its implementation might imply a certain degree of mistrust vis-à-vis lobbyists.[392]

As the JTRS Staff explains, not everyone in the EP *de facto* applies the TR.[393] Likewise, the MEP admits that his office staff also does not check registries for background information about every lobbyist he considers to meet.[394] In an effort to raise awareness among those who should apply the TR regularly and to fulfill the responsibility that has been conferred to it by the IIA,[395] the JTRS

---

[386] Europa (2012).
[387] JTRS (2012b), 2.2.
[388] WWF Employee. (2013). Interview of May 28, 2013.
[389] BUSINESSEUROPE Employee. (2013). Interview of July 3, 2013.
[390] DLR Employee (2013).
[391] JTRS Staff (2013a).
[392] BDI Employee. (2013). Interview of June 19, 2013.
[393] JTRS Staff (2013a).
[394] The MEP (2013).
[395] European Parliament (2011), VII 24.

offers workshops to MEP assistants. The Secretariat aims to promote the register as a helpful and essential daily tool to provide 'concise' information about interest representatives seeking to lobby the EU. In 2012, three such workshops were conducted in the Parliament, each of which involved 40–50 participants.[396] Considering that the parliamentary assembly by the accession of Croatia has grown to 766 MEPs, the amount of workshops concluded seems insufficient and, therefore, ineffective in its reach. However, in addition to the workshops mentioned, the TR's Secretariat encourages parliamentary staff to promote registration among nonregistrants, and promotes the TR itself through its Head of Secretariat, Gérard Legris, for instance through public talks.[397]

Even if ALTER-EU concluded in its latest report that a major amount of "larger Brussels-based lobby consultancies" had registered already,[398] professional consultancies and law firms are still rather hesitant to join the TR. However, with regard to the latest figures the general target of the JTRS to increase the number of registrants can be assessed as realized.[399] Moreover, the past criticism concerning entities absent from the register has not always proved to be justified, because some registrants might not have been found due to a failure in search, such as by misspelling or incorrect abbreviations used. Overall, the number of registrants rose especially between the TR's implementation and May/June 2012, with this timeframe being the official transition period for former ROIR registrants. Afterwards, numbers continued to increase, although to a smaller degree. Since a major amount of these registrants faces difficulties with registration requirements, revision is essential. Finally, awareness-raising measures by the JTRS are identified as a step in the right direction to promote the TR, but should be intensified.

3.2 The United States of America

3.2.1 Implementation of the Lobbying Disclosure Act

Lobbying registration in the United States "encompasses binding laws and regulations [...] applicable to all individuals or institutions engaging in lobbying activities."[400] Pursuant to Krajewski, the system under the LDA is, therefore, an

---

[396] JTRS Staff (Interview 2013a).
[397] Ibid.
[398] ALTER-EU (2013), p. 8.
[399] See also Gentili (2013), p. 14.
[400] Krajewski (2013a), p. 6.

example for **mandatory legislation**.[401] As defined by the LDA guidance, a lobbyist is an individual employed or retained by a client for financial or other compensation for services, establishing **more than one lobbying** contact, and whose services during a three-month period are by **20 percent** dedicated to lobbying activities.[402] Therefore, a lobbying firm is required to register with the databases as soon as the working time of one of its employees exceeds this threshold.[403] Furthermore, the LDA defines terms as *agency, client, covered executive branch official, and covered legislative branch official, employee, foreign entity, lobbying activities, lobbying contact, lobbying firm, lobbyist, media organization, Member of Congress, organization, person or entity, public official,* as well as *State*.[404] A client, for example, is identified as any person or entity "that employs or retains another person for financial or other compensation to conduct lobbying activities on behalf of that person or entity." If an organization employs its own lobbyists, for reporting purposes it is considered as its own client.[405] An organization is considered by the LDA as a person or entity other than an individual.[406] A person or entity can be an individual, corporation, company, foundation, association, labor organization, firm, partnership, society, joint stock company, group of organizations, or State or local government.[407] As a matter of principle, the 20 percent threshold applies already to registration in general and not just to the reporting section.[408]

⊃ **Who is expected to register?**

With regard to the definition laid down in the LDA, a registrant can either be a **lobbying firm** or a **lobbying organization**.[409] An entity is perceived as a **lobbying firm** as soon as it is composed of one or more individuals serving as a lobbyist for a client outside that firm;[410] the scope of this definition also includes **self-employed lobbyists**.[411] Conversely, lobbying organizations employ their

---

[401] Ibid.
[402] Office of the Clerk. (2013a). Lobbying Disclosure Act Guidance. http://lobbyingdisclosure.house.gov/amended_lda_guide.html, visited on March 29, 2013, s. 3.
[403] Holman and Luneburg (2012).
[404] LDA of 1995. (2007). http://www.senate.gov/legislative/Lobbying/Lobby_Disclosure_Act/compilation.pdf, visited on May 19, 2013, s. 3.
[405] Office of the Clerk (2013a). s. 3.
[406] LDA of 1995 (2007), s. 3 (13).
[407] Ibid., s. 3 (14).
[408] Office of the Clerk (2013a), s. 4.
[409] Office of the Clerk (2013a). s. 3.
[410] Ibid.
[411] Ibid.

own in-house lobbyists.[412] Single lobbyists are considered as a lobbying firm if they are self-employed.[413] Under the LDA, a registrant shall register with the SOS and the CHR no later than **45 days** after a first lobbying contact is made or a lobbyist is employed or retained to establish such a contact.[414] As a matter of principle, any organization employing one or more persons for lobbying activities is obliged to file a single registration "on behalf of such employees for each client on whose behalf the employees act as lobbyist."[415] However, those clients are not necessarily obliged to submit reports on their own.[416] In case a lobbying firm establishes several contacts for a single client, a single registration for the particular client is sufficient.[417] Exemptions for registration exist for lobbying firms whose total income related to lobbying activities on behalf of a client does not exceed a quarterly amount of $3,000,[418] and for lobbying organizations whose total expenses do not aggregate to more than $12,500 during a quarterly period.[419] Even if the definition of lobbying contacts does not include communications by a church, if the latter or an integrated auxiliary, a convention or association of churches, or a religious order hires an external lobbying firm to conduct lobbying activities on its behalf, the outside firm is required to register.[420]

◯ **Which activities are concerned by the scope of the register?**

Lobbying activities under the LDA cover lobbying contacts and efforts supporting them: This may include preparation and planning of activities, research and background work, as well as the coordination with lobbying activities of others.[421] Lobbying contacts include any oral, written, or electronic communication on behalf of a client,[422] which is directed toward an executive branch

---

[412] Ibid. s. 4.
[413] Ibid.
[414] Ibid., s. 4 (a)(1), (2).
[415] LDA of 1995 (2007), s. 4 (a)(2).
[416] CHR Employee (2013).
[417] LDA, s. 4(c).
[418] Office of the Clerk (2013a), s. 2.
[419] LDA, s. 4 (a)(3); Since 1997, these two amounts need being updated every four years to reflect changes in the Consumer Price Index.
[420] Office of the Clerk (2013a), s. 5.
[421] Ibid., s. 3(7).
[422] Ibid., s. 3.

official[423] or a covered legislative branch official[424] focusing on the formulation, modification, or adoption of Federal legislation and legislative proposals.[425]

◯ **Which information is expected to be disclosed?**

Registration with the US register requires submitting the name, address, business telephone number, principal place of the registrant's business, and a general description of business or activities. Except for a telephone number the same data are due to be entered for each of the registrant's clients,[426] as well as for any organization other than the client contributing more than $5,000 to the registrant's or the client's quarterly lobbying activities and that actively participates, plans, supervises, or controls such lobbying activities.[427] Other essential information is the name, address, principal place of business, the amount of any contribution of more than $5,000 to the lobbying activities of the registrant, and the approximate percentage of equitable ownership for any foreign entity holding a minimum of 20 percent ownership in the client, and which participates in the client's activities or is affiliated with the latter. The LDA does not only oblige registrants to name every employee who has already acted or is expected to act as a lobbyist for a client, but moreover determines to list the position of any of these employees in case they served as a covered executive or legislative branch official within a period of 20 years before the particular employee acted for the first time as a lobbyist on behalf of the registrant's client.[428]

---

[423] Definition as of LDA s. 3(4): a Member of Congress; an elected officer of either House of Congress; any employee of, or any other individual functioning in the capacity of an employee of a Member of Congress; a committee of either House of Congress; the leadership staff of the House of Representatives or the leadership staff of the Senate; a joint committee of Congress; and a working group or caucus organized to provide legislative services or other assistance to Members of Congress; and any other legislative branch employee serving in a position described under section 109 (13) of the Ethics in Government Act of 1978 (5 U.S.C. App.).

[424] Definition as of LDA s. 3(3): the President; the Vice President; any officer or employee, or any other individual functioning in the capacity of such an officer or employee, in the Executive Office of the President; any officer or employee serving in a position in level I, II, III, IV, or V of the Executive Schedule, as designated by statute or Executive order; any member of the uniformed services whose pay grade is at or above 0-7 under section 201 of title 37, United States Code; and any officer or employee serving in a position of a confidential, policy-determining, policy-making, or policy advocating character described in section 7511(b)(2) of title 5, United States Code.

[425] LDA of 1995 (2007), s. 3(8).
[426] Ibid., s. 4(b)(1), (2).
[427] Ibid., s. 4(b)(3).
[428] Ibid., s. 4(b)(6).

Registration needs to be complemented by a statement of the "general issue areas" the registrant plans to lobby, as well as of specific legislative issues that have already been targeted by lobbying activities.[429] Each registrant is obliged to electronically file quarterly reports to the SOS and the CHR no later than **20 days** after a quarterly period's ending (beginning on the first day of January, April, July, and October) about its lobbying activities and related expenses made during the quarter concerned.[430] The requirement for listing a lobbying firm's clients is linked to a necessary identification "of whether the client is a State or local government or a department, agency, special purpose district" or other entity controlled by state or local governments.[431] As long as the registrant remains listed in the databases, lobbying activities must be continuously reported even if they would not "trigger a registration requirement in the first instance."[432]

Reports need to contain the following elements: name of the registrant and client; changes or updates to the information provided in initial registration; for each 'general issue area' a list of bill numbers and references to specific executive branch actions, statements of the Houses of Congress and the Federal agencies contacted by lobbyists that are employed by the registrant, listed employees of the registrant acting as lobbyists, and a description of interests of foreign entities in the organization or firm.[433] In addition, lobbying firms need to reveal an estimate of the total amount of gross income related to lobbying activities on behalf of their clients. In case the registrant conducts lobbying activities on its own behalf, "a good faith estimate of the total expenses" with regard to lobbying activities in the quarterly period concerned is expected to be submitted as well. Estimated amounts exceeding $5,000 are expected to be rounded to the nearest $10,000. In case they are not in excess of $5,000, registrants have to confirm this by an included statement.[434] Reports filed under this category are also referred to as 'LD-2 forms' (activity-related and financial reports, United States). Initial registration is filed through 'LD-1 forms.'[435]

---

[429] Ibid., s. 4(b)(5).
[430] Magloff, L. (2013). Federal Lobbying Guidelines. http://smallbusiness.chron.com/federal-lobbying-guidelines-14110.html, visited on March 31, 2013.
[431] LDA of 1995 (2007), s. 5(b)(4),(5).
[432] Office of the Clerk (2013a), s. 6.
[433] LDA of 1995 (2007), s. 5(b).
[434] Ibid., s. 5(c)(1),(2).
[435] Office of the Clerk (2013a), s. 3.

No later than **30 days** after a semiannual period's ending on the first day of January and July of each year, lobbying firms and organizations shall submit a report on certain contributions with the CHR and the SOS. Reports are determined to contain the date, recipient, and exact funds contributed to Federal candidates or officeholders, leadership PAC, or political party committees, if the funding through a semiannual period is equal to or exceeds $200. In addition, reports need to cover the date, names of honorees and payees, and the sum of funds paid for events to honor or recognize covered legislative or executive branch officials; to entities named for or in recognition of such officials; for a meeting, retreat, conference, or similar event held by such officials; to Presidential library foundations and Presidential inaugural committees; as well as the date, recipient, name of covered officials, the payees, and sum of funds paid to an entity established, financed, maintained, or controlled by such officials.[436] Registrants must continue to list lobbyists employed by them as 'active' as long as they expect them to fall under the scope of lobbying activities during the recent or following quarter.[437] Moreover, registrants and their lobbying employees are obliged to report separately.[438] Since the obligation to file reports on certain contributions was implemented by section 203, HLOGA, these documents are referred to as 'LD-203 reports.'

Although lobbyists are further obliged to report their contacts in their reports, the law does not determine that they have to list contact persons by name—reporting the respective political body is sufficient. In addition to reporting the legislative or executive institution they approached, the LDA requires them to list the legislative subject of their conversation.[439] Registrations and reports need to be publicly available online and accessible without any charge.[440] As the CHR Employee points out, registrants under the LDA are neither granted any special privileges, nor do they have to show a special ID when accessing facilities of the Congress: Offices of Congressmen and Senators can individually decide about how to handle access, but he would not be surprised if special access passes formed part of registration in the future, adding that this required a change of law.[441]

---

[436] Ibid., s. 7.
[437] Ibid., s. 8.
[438] LDA of 1995 (2007), s. 5(d)(1)(A),(B),(C),(D); Office of the Clerk. (2013b). Notifications and Announcements. http://lobbyingdisclosure.house.gov/, visited on April 13, 2013.
[439] CHR Employee (2013).
[440] LDA of 1995 (2007), s. 6(a)(9).
[441] CHR Employee (2013).

Compared to the TR, registration in the United States does not oblige to agree on a code of conduct. However, lobbyists can potentially be considered liable for enabling or enhancing breaches of the congressional ethics rules by Members of Congress. Instead of ticking a box for their agreement, lobbyists in the United States have to "certify in writing on a special semi-annual report that they have read the rules of the Senate and House of Representatives" on gift and travel restrictions, understood them, and not knowingly violated them in the past.[442] Once a report is submitted, a copy is sent to both databases.[443] After all reports are filed to a certain deadline ending, registrations are reviewed to avoid duplicates. As a matter of logic, the extent of reports rises with every quarterly or semiannual deadline approaching. However, the CHR does not provide quarterly, but instantaneous figures. It is assumed that databases of the SOS and the CHR are accessed by citizens rather than by the Congress, while political organizations and watchdogs are also expected to monitor registration on a regular basis.[444] Registrations and reports need to be retained for at least six years.[445] Registration can be terminated if the registrant is no longer employed or retained to carry out lobbying activities, but the SOS and the CHR need to be notified about this change of procedure.[446] Proper termination requires registrants to remove the name of the terminating lobbyist from every report filed for its clients.[447]

As a mandatory registration system, the US lobby register is often even referred to as a model system. Due to its obligatory conception, legislation incorporates thresholds as the amount of contacts, percentage of time related to lobbying, or deadlines by amount of days or fixed dates. These clear and precise thresholds support the feasibility of the system as such, since at first sight they seem applicable to all actors. Complementarily, the LDA defines several other actors or activities, which is not only an indicator for governmental attempts to avoid misinterpretations, but also reflects again that lobbying regulation in the United States has been redefined, amended, and improved several times. Equally, the amount of definitions implies that US legislators take lobbying as an accepted business. Since registration with the databases is required by law, privileges—such as access passes—are simply not required.

---

[442] Holman and Luneburg (2012).
[443] CHR Employee (2013).
[444] Ibid.
[445] LDA of 1995 (2007), s. 6(5).
[446] Ibid., s. 4(d).
[447] Office of the Clerk (2013), s. 8.

3.2.2 Legal basis

As already outlined, lobbying registration in the United States is based on the regulation of the LDA amended through HLOGA. The Congress justified the LDA's adoption by the underlying assumption that "responsible representative Government requires public awareness of the efforts of paid lobbyists to influence the public decision making process" of governmental legislative and executive branches.[448] A second listed reason was that Congress considered existing lobbying disclosure regulations as ineffective due to

> unclear statutory language, weak administrative and enforcement provisions, and an absence of clear guidance as to who is required to register and what they are required to disclose.[449]

Consequently, this statement implies that the US government had been clearly aware of deficits in previous lobbying regulations. In addition, the LDA was intended to "increase public confidence in the integrity of Government."[450] In 2007, the LDA was amended by HLOGA, which was not a "law onto itself" but a legislative act including provisions to amend various laws,[451] and became effective on January 1, 2008.[452] Since the fundamental rights of US citizens to petition, associate, and express their personal opinions are protected through the LDA by the ruling that "Nothing in this Act shall be construed to prohibit or interfere with" these rights, they still prevail after the adoption of the Bill of Rights in 1791.[453]

The amendments of the LDA through HLOGA are another example for the legislative tradition of the United States to regularly revise and redefine its lobbying regulations. Furthermore, HLOGA can be assessed as an indicator that already after 12 years of the LDA's implementation, lobbying activities in the United States and their intensity had changed to a degree that made an update of current legislation essential. Maximizing the civil fine from $50,000 to $200,000 is certainly an indicator for an increased pressure for lobbyists to generally comply with the LDA and make available their information properly and timely.

---

[448] LDA of 1995 (2997), s. 2(1).
[449] Ibid., s. 2(2).
[450] LDA of 1995 (2007), s. 2(3).
[451] US Watchdog Representative. (2013). E-mail received on May 21, 2013.
[452] Straus, J.R. (2008). Honest Leadership and Open Government Act of 2007: The Role of the Clerk of the House and Secretary of the Senate. http://www.fas.org/sgp/crs/secrecy/RL34377.pdf, visited on August 2, 2013.
[453] LDA of 1995 (2007), s. 8(a)(1)(2)(3).

3.2.3 Instruments of control and penalties

Lobbying registration in the United States incorporates several levels and measures of control as well as sanctions, which are, due to the legislative obligation to register, a lot stricter than in the EU. The SOS and the CHR are obliged to provide guidance and assistance on registration and reporting under the LDA and to "develop common standards, rules, and procedures for compliance with this Act." An example for guidance is the semiannually published LDA Guidance. As further determined, the institutions are required to "review, [...] verify and inquire to ensure the accuracy, completeness, and timeliness of registration and reports."[454] Furthermore, it is their duty to make registrations and reports available online for "public inspection."[455] As an additional obligation, the SOS and the CHR shall notify registrants as soon as they do not comply with rules of the LDA.[456] If the notified registrant fails to provide an appropriate response within 60 days, the SOS and the CHR are obliged to inform the US Attorney General for the District of Columbia about the issue.[457]

The latter is liable for submitting semiannual reports to the congressional committees[458] about the amount of enforcement actions and sentences taken and imposed by the Department of Justice and holds the "sole power to seek court sanctions for violations."[459] However, such reports are prohibited to contain names of individuals concerned or information enabling to identify such individuals, unless they have already been published by public record.[460] The SOS and the CHR make the amount of noncompliant registrants publicly available every six months.[461] The scope of responsibility of the SOS and the CHR remains generally limited to "referral authority"[462] since neither body is allowed to investigate or audit lobbyists.[463]

---

[454] Ibid., s. 6(a)(1),(2).
[455] Ibid., s. 6(a)(4).
[456] Levin, R.M. (2011). Lobbying Law in the Spotlight: 'Challenges and Proposed Improvements Report of the Task Force on Federal Lobbying Laws'. Section of Administrative Law and Regulatory Practice American Bar Association. http://www.americanbar.org/content/dam/aba/migrated/2011_build/administrative_law/lobbying_task_force_report_01 0311.authcheckdam.pdf, visited on May 13, 2013, p. 5.
[457] LDA of 1995 (2007), s. 6(a)(8).
[458] Committee on Homeland Security and Governmental Affairs, the Committee on the Judiciary of the Senate, the Committee on the Judiciary of the House of Representatives.
[459] Holman and Luneburg (2012).
[460] LDA of 1995 (2007), s. 6 (b)(2).
[461] Ibid., s. 6(a)(11).
[462] CHR Employee (2013).
[463] LDA of 1995 (2007), s. 8(c).

The US Government Accountability Office (GAO) functions as an 'auditory arm,' which is mandated by law to audit all reports and registrations filed, and forms part of the government's legislative branch. As its director, the Comptroller General is endowed with the responsibility to "audit the extent of compliance or noncompliance with the requirements [...] by lobbyists, lobbying firms, and registrants." Considering a random sampling of registrations and reports, the report of GAO contains the Comptroller General's assessment of matters of noncompliance, and recommendations for improving compliance of lobbyists, lobbying firms, and registrants, with reference to the US Attorney. As further ruled, the report is determined to provide the Department of Justice with the necessary resources and authorities for the enforcement of the act.[464] In case an individual or an entity fails to submit a report, the SOS and the HOR can inform the US Attorney, which would then commence further investigations.[465] If the registrant knowingly fails to "remedy a defective filing" or to comply with any other requirement of the LDA within **60 days** after notice by the SOS and the CHR, a civil fine of up to $200,000 as well as imprisonment of up to five years can be imposed, depending on the violation's extent and gravity.[466]

From 1995 to 2007, undisclosed financial amounts of registrants led to three enforcement cases settled by the US Attorney's Office. After HLOGA was implemented, the Attorney's office entered into negotiated settlements three times: Once in 2011 ($45,000) and twice in 2012 ($50,000 and $30,000). Consequently, under the LDA as amended by HLOGA the highest monetary penalty was settled at $50,000. In June 2013, the US Attorney's Office filed a complaint against a consulting firm for violations of the LDA that was linked to fines of up to $33 million. Seemingly, the registrant had ignored several previous notifications from the SOS, the CHR, and the Attorney. As of the current state of knowledge of the CHR Employee, the criminal penalty of imprisonment has not yet been imposed in the United States.[467] In total, the SOS has referred 11,906 violations to the Attorney since 1995, whereas GAO has audited more than a thousand LDA filings since the implementation of HLOGA.[468]

---

[464] Ibid., s. 26(a),(b)(1).
[465] CHR Employee (2013).
[466] LDA of 1995 (2007), s. 7(1), (2); Magloff (2013); In addition to that, the registrant can also be fined under title 18 according to the US Code (USC).
[467] CHR Employee (2013).
[468] DeLacy, C. and Irving J.S. IV (2013). US Attorney Seeks $33 Million Lobbying Disclosure Act Penalty. Complaint Signals a More Aggressive Enforcement Policy. http://www.hklaw.com/publications/US-Attorney-Seeks-33-Million-Lobbying-Disclosure-Act-Penalty-06-13-2013/, visited on August 4, 2013.

In its current report of April 2013,[469] GAO estimates that 97 percent of examined LD-2 reports provided documentation to support reported income and expenses, 85 percent filed contribution reports (LD-203) as required[470] with only a minimum of six percent failing to disclose contributions.[471] Moreover, 15 percent of LD-2 reports lacked proper disclosure of previously held covered positions. New registrants complied with LDA regulations to a major degree: 90 percent of new registrants submitted disclosure reports as expected.[472] As of March 2013, the Office of the Attorney had received 2,062 complaints from the SOS and the CHR about noncompliance with LD-2 reports and 2,472 referrals for incorrect LD-203 reports, related to reporting periods of 2009, 2010, 2011, and 2012.[473] Eight registrants were contacted by the Office of the US Attorney due to repeated failure for filing reports as required, of which four submitted overdue reports or terminated registration after notifying measures were taken. Subsequently, the Attorney agreed on the aforementioned monetary penalties of $30,000 and $50,000, respectively, which both firms paid in March 2013.[474] Nevertheless, the American Bar Association concluded that surveillance of the LDA does not lead to "formal enforcement actions," which in turn leads to noncompliance by lobbyists with regulations.[475]

Considering lobbying disclosure, the SOS and the CHR equally function as guiding and assisting bodies in charge of guaranteeing the availability and accessibility of lobbyists' registrations and reports to the public and governmental agencies in charge of control. However, its responsibilities of enforcement remain limited to measures of notification, which can still be identified as the first level of control. The second level is formed by both the US Attorney, as the single power authorized to seek court sanctions, and GAO as auditing instance. The final level of enforcement consists of the Department of Justice.

---

[469] Review regards "a random sample of 100 quarterly disclosure LD-2 reports filed for the third and fourth quarters of calendar year 2011 and the first and second quarters of calendar year 2012," as well as "two random samples totaling 160 LD-203 reports from year-end 2011 and midyear 2012."
[470] The US GAO. (2013). 2012 Lobbying Disclosure. Observations on Lobbyists' Compliance with Disclosure Requirements. http://www.gao.gov/assets/660/653471.pdf, visited on August 4, 2013, Highlights page.
[471] Ibid., p. 12.
[472] Ibid., p. 13.
[473] Ibid., pp. 18, 20.
[474] The US GAO (2013), Highlights page.
[475] EU Observer. (2013). EU Losing Again in Lobbying Game. http://euobserver.com/opinion/119528, visited on April 27, 2013.

Nevertheless, the system still lacks an external agency of enforcement. Reportedly, registrants mainly fulfill registration and reporting criteria; mistakes and noncompliance remain at a minor degree. This could be an indicator for lobbyists' respect for the disclosure system, or a set of registration requirements that is overly clear. With regard to the $ 33-million fine, the US Attorney obviously aggregated overdue penalties of the consultancy concerned. Since previous settlements were all negotiated, this can be considered as an indicator for "a more aggressive LDA enforcement policy."[476]

3.2.4 Effectiveness and criticism

As of July 3, 2013, the database of the House of Representatives counted 4,744 'registrants' as registered unique organizations. In total, these registrants employ a number of 13,853 lobbyists working on behalf of 16,749 clients. The most current available figures of the SOS date back to September 30, 2012 and counted 4,574 registrants, 12,564 lobbyists, and 17,258 clients. Despite the obligation for lobbyists to report to both databases, registers of the SOS and the CHR do not necessarily show the same figures in the end.[477] One can infer from this result that registrations and reports might be handled differently, as with regard to the avoidance of double counting or the consideration of terminations—even if both databases belong to one single system. Despite the fact that electronic submission of a report leads to a copy being sent to both databases, the CHR Employee points out that the HOR uploads forms faster than the SOS: "the Senate does their thing and the House does ours."[478] According to the US Watchdog Representative, the reason for the maintenance of two registers still remains unclear.[479] As of July 29, 2013, the CRP counted 10,290 lobbyists. To generate its published figures, CRP downloads individual records filed by each lobbyist on lobbying activities and adjusts them to avoid double counting.[480]

---

[476] DeLacy and Irving (2013).
[477] CHR Employee (2013).
[478] CHR Employee (2013).
[479] US Watchdog Representative. (2013a). E-mail received on May 21, 2013.
[480] CRP Representative. (2013a). E-mail received on June 3, 2013.

Figure 2. Number of US lobbyists[481]

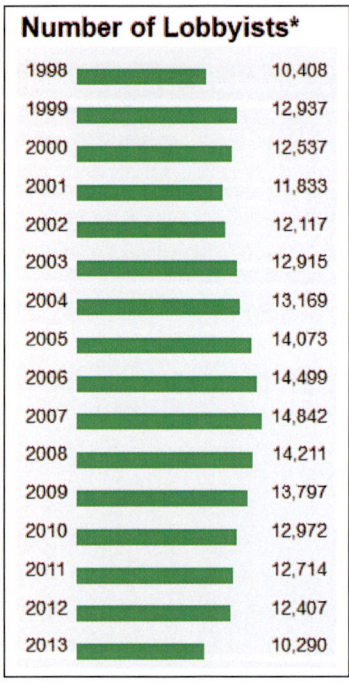

However, the CHR Employee also points out that "inactive totals" are not considered in the counts made by the CHR.[482] This still does not explain why results of the CHR and the CRP do not resemble each other. The number of lobbyists as exposed by the CRP in Figure 2 shows that numbers counted between 1998 and 2013 have always reflected the average of 12,857 lobbyists to a certain degree. Furthermore, even after the implementation of HLOGA no major changes can be identified. The US Watchdog Representative considers the number of registered lobbyists in the United States a "more or less [.] realistic reflection of the actual number of lobbyists."[483] Since interest representatives disclose their reports and identify themselves as lobbyists by that, they meet the criteria and intention of the LDA. Therefore, the CHR Employee considers lobbying registration in the United States a success.[484]

As a matter of fact, the US registration system is composed of the LDA Disclosure Database and the Lobbying Contributions Database.[485] Despite his positive conclusion about lobbyist counts, the US Watchdog Representative criticizes that information remains limited to general data about lobbyists, a company or an industry—full informative capacity of the particular database can only be accessed by downloading the latter into one's own data program.[486] As the US Watchdog Representative further explains, user search results do not show information about lobbying persons, time of lobbying, amounts spent on

---

[481] Center for Responsive Politics. (2013). Lobbying Database. http://www.opensecrets.org/lobby/, visited on May 26, 2013; Data for the most recent year was downloaded on July 29, 2013.
[482] CHR Employee (2013).
[483] US Watchdog Representative (2013a).
[484] CHR Employee (2013).
[485] Office of the Clerk. 113th Congress. 1st Session. Public Disclosure. http://clerk.house.gov/public_disc/index.aspx, visited on August 5, 2013.
[486] US Watchdog Representative. (2013b). E-mail received on May 26, 2013.

such activities, specific bill, or issue areas[487]. With regard to the information provided by simple search (without downloading databases), research for quarterly reports shows the registrant's and client's name, the filing type (first/second/third/fourth-quarter report), amount reported, the date of submission as well as the filing year. Searching contribution reports reveals the registrant's as well as the lobbyist's name, the filing type (year-end/mid-year report), the date of posting, and the year of filing.[488] Compared to information provided by the EU's TR, the degree of accessible data remains therefore low. As the CRP Representative further explains, using acronyms of registrants' names to search the Senate's databases does not lead to results: Names or parts of the names necessarily have to be typed correctly to find the entry required since the search program does not tolerate spelling mistakes.[489]

As a recent GAO survey among LDA registrants revealed, most lobbyists identified reporting requirements for LD-2 reporting as "very easy" or "somewhat easy." Categories assessed most easy to provide information for were "terminating lobbyists" (52 percent said 'very easy'), "covered positions" (51 percent said 'very easy'), and "issue codes" (47 percent said 'very easy'). Only a few faced problems, such as to distinguish between lobbying and nonlobbying activities (23 percent said 'somewhat difficult or very difficult') or to list previous covered positions of their employees (22 percent).[490] Therefore, at least for LD-2 reporting the requirements seem understandable and easy to realize. After the Office of the US Attorney developed a system to track lobbyists with a history of chronic noncompliance and repeated failure to disclose reports, reportedly more noncompliant lobbyists could be identified for civil enforcement action through this complementary tool.[491] Even if Holman underlines that HLOGA made the LDA "disclosure regime [...] more frequent, more thorough, and more readily available to the public on the Internet,"[492] the scholar criticizes that registration in the United States still excludes activities of grassroots lobbying.[493] As the CHR Employee assumes, there is a certain reason for this: Most individuals or entities applying grassroots tactics refer to charitable "public

---

[487] Holman (2008), p. 10.
[488] See Annex.
[489] CRP Representative. (2013b). E-mail received on June 21, 2013.
[490] GAO (2013), p. 16.
[491] GAO (2013), p. 22.
[492] Holman (2008), p. 11
[493] US Watchdog Representative (2013a); see also Thunert (^{1}2003), p. 331.

style organisations" that are based on membership and can justify their activities by the right to petition Members of Congress. The CHR Employee would "tend to agree with the exception."[494]

With reference to CRP figures, lobbying numbers in the United States seem stable, even if current governmental figures and those of the watchdog do not resemble each other. Generally, measuring the effectiveness and efficiency of the US registration system seems, therefore, rather difficult in terms of comparing the amount of registrants. Also with regard to the effectiveness of LDA search engines, users might be left in confusion: Spelling mistakes leading to no search results might cause the assumption that a certain lobbyist, client, or registrant has simply not registered or remained inactive during the quarter concerned. Even if diverging databases and different tally results are not understandable, the LDA as amended does not provide a provision ruling that uniform methods and instruments need to be applied. While full information about registrants can only be accessed by downloading the particular database, the data available online only provide the user with a minimum degree of information compared to entries in the TR. In addition, critics point to the LDA's exclusion of grassroots lobbying and the lack of a single agency in charge of handling measures of enforcement.[495] Consequently, also the US register is still imperfect, not overall effective or efficient, and its applicability as model lobby regulation needs to be questioned.

---

[494] CHR Employee (2013).
[495] Wilson et al. ([12]2011), p. 281; US Watchdog Representative (2013a); CHR Employee (2013).

4 Result subsumption, discussion, and perspectives

The following sections will answer the research questions of this book, evaluate the research method after its implementation, and identify approaches for future research related to lobbying registration.

4.1 Conclusion on the comparison

Table 4. Comparison overview (provides the main differences and similarities of both registers)

Category	EU TR (2011)	US LDA (2007, as amended)
Legal basis	Nonlegal interinstitutional agreement; legal basis not officially confirmed by EU; possibility: Article 298 TFEU with doctrine of implemented acts	LDA as amended by HLOGA
Official operator(s)	EP, European Commission represented by the JTRS	SOS, CHR
Constitution	Voluntary/Free of charge/Web interface	Mandatory/Free of charge/Web interface
Target group for registration	All organizations and self-employed individuals engaged in activities of the register's scope: (I) Professional consultancies/law firms/self-employed consultants; (II) In-house lobbyists and trade/professional associations; (III) NGOs; (IV) Think tanks, research and academic institutions; (V) Organizations representing churches and religious communities; (VI) Organizations representing local, regional, and municipal authorities, other public or mixed entities, etc.; Clients of consultancies, law firms and self-employed consultants	Lobbying firms, lobbying organizations, self-employed lobbyists, NGOs other than churches Clients not per law required to register or report

Target group for application	EU public officials and personnel, interest representatives, EU citizens (including media, academics, watchdogs, etc.)	Citizens, Congress, political organizations, watchdogs
Exemption from registration	EU Member States governments; governments of third countries; international intergovernmental organizations and their diplomatic missions; churches; political parties; local, municipal, and regional authorities	Lobbying firms whose total income related to lobbying activities on behalf of a client is not >$3,000 quarterly; lobbying organizations whose total expenses are not aggregating to >$12,500 quarterly
	Their representative offices, legal bodies, and associations conducting lobbying activities vis-à-vis the EU are required to register	If churches, integrated auxiliaries, a convention, association of churches, or religious orders hire lobbying firm: Outside firm required to register
Included definitions	*Lobbyist:* Organizations and self-employed individuals engaging in activities with the objective of influencing the decision-making processes of the EU	*Lobbyist:* Individual, employed or retained by a client for financial or different compensation, providing services including more than one lobbying contact, lobbying activities account for more than 20 percent of the employee's time to a client during a three-month period
	Other terms: /	*Other terms*: Agency, client, covered executive branch official and covered legislative branch official, employee, foreign entity, lobbying activities, lobbying contact, lobbying firm, lobbyist, media organization, Member of Congress, organization, person or entity, public official, state

	Lobbying activities: All activities [...] carried out with the objective of directly or indirectly influencing the formulation or implementation of policy and the decision-making processes of the EU institutions; contacting members, officials or other staff of EU institutions; irrespective of the channel or medium used *Lobbying contacts:* Preparing, circulating, and communicating letters, information material, or discussion papers and position papers, and organizing events, meetings, or promotional activities and social events or conferences; invitations which have been sent to Members, officials or other staff of the EU institutions; participation in formal consultations; contacts can be established through outsourcing; media itself; think tanks; platforms; forum; campaigns; grassroots initiatives; voluntary contributions and participation in formal consultations on EU legislation	*Lobbying activities:* Lobbying contacts and any effort supporting such contacts, including preparation, planning, research, and other necessary background work of such activities intended and performed for being used in such contacts and coordination with lobbying activities of others *Lobbying contacts:* Any oral or written (electronic) communication to a covered executive branch official or a covered legislative branch official on behalf of a client focusing on the formulation, modification, or adoption of Federal legislation, Federal rule, regulation, Executive order, or any other program, policy, or position of the US Government, administration or executive of a Federal program or policy, nomination or confirmation of a person for a position subject to confirmation by the Senate
Information required	*Contact information:* Name of the organization, address, phone number, e-mail address, and website; person legally responsible for organization; organization's director or managing partner or principal contact point with respect to activities covered by the register; name of access pass holders	*Contact information:* Name, address, business telephone number, principal place of business, general description of business or activities required for registrant, clients, and any organization other than the client contributing more than $5,000 to the registrant's semiannual lobbying activities, and partially or totally planning, supervising and controlling such lobbying activities; Name, address, principal place of business, amount of any contribution of >$5,000 to the lobbying activities of the registrant and equitable ownership exceeding a share of 20 percent

	in the client or client's affiliate of any foreign entity, or that participates in the client's activities or is itself affiliated with the latter
Activity information: Number of persons involved in relevant activities; goals/remit; fields of interest; activities; countries of operation; affiliations to networks, number of members (individuals and organizations, if applicable)	*Activity information:* Names of registrant's employees having acted or being expected to act as lobbyist on behalf of a client; position served as executive or legislative branch official 20 years before becoming active as a lobbyist; 'general issue area' information such as a list of bill numbers and references to specific executive branch actions; a statement of the Houses of Congress and the Federal agencies who have been contacted by lobbyists employed by the registrant; a description of interests of foreign entities; Name of the lobbied political body by its institution, legislative subject of conversation; A list of lobbying firms' clients linked to necessary identification "of whether the client is a state or local government or a department, agency, special purpose district" or other entity controlled by state or local governments; clients to be identified as foreign entities
Financial information: Professional consultancies, law firms, and self-employed consultants to disclose details on turnover and "relative weight attaching to their clients"; details to be submitted in bracket sizes: €50,000 for €0–499,000, €100,000 for €500,000–€1,000,000, and €250,000 for sums greater than €1,000,000; clients' obligation to declare	*Financial information:* Lobbying firms to reveal an estimate of the total amount of gross income related to lobbying activities on behalf of its clients; registrant conducting lobbying activities on their own behalf required to submit "a good faith estimate of the total expenses" with regard to lobbying activities;

	their own contractual activities in their registries; In-house lobbyists, trade and professional associations required to base their estimates on their expenses related to lobbying activities; registrants of sections III–VI have to additionally list their overall budget including breakdown of main sources of funding; all required to list amount and source of EU funding	Estimated amounts exceeding $5,000 to be rounded to the nearest $10,000; if amount not greater than $5,000, registrants' notification about this is required. Date, recipient, and exact funds contributed to Federal candidates or officeholders, leadership PAC, or political party committees, if funding through semiannual period equal to or exceeding $200; Date, names of honorees and payees, sum of funds paid for events of honor or recognition, entities named for or in recognition of such officials; to Presidential library foundations and Presidential inaugural committees; paid to an entity established, financed, maintained, controlled by such officials
Required updating	At least once a year	Activity-related and financial reports (LD-2): Quarterly updates; certain contributions reports (LD-203): Semiannual updates
	Deadlines: Not defined	*Deadlines:* Registration no later than **45 days** after first lobbying contact; activity reports no later than **20 days** to the quarter ended, certain contributions reports no later than **30 days** to the semiannual period ended; reports to be filed for every single client
Granted privileges	EP access passes, alerting service for Commission's roadmaps, and public consultations	-
Linked requirements	Acceptance of a code of conduct	Written certification that registrant has read, understood, and not violated rules of the Senate and House of Representatives on gift and travel restrictions

Controlling institution	JTRS	First level: SOS and CHR; second level: GAO and US Attorney; third level: Department of Justice
	Degree of control: Quality checks random-like and after alerts/complaints; 404 quality checks from March–September 2012	*Degree of control:* Obligation of GAO and CHR to review reports; 2,062 complaints about noncompliance with LD-2 reports; 2,472 complaints about incorrect LD-203 reports for the years 2009, 2010, 2011, and 2012
Instruments of control	Random quality checks, complaints, alerts by JTRS and public	Compliance checks by SOS and CHR; random auditing through GAO
Complaint mechanism	Public complaints possible	Complaints limited to SOS and CHR
Penalties	For unintended and immediately corrected inaccuracies, JTRS **notifies in written form** and asks for correction, no public notification; deliberate noncompliance as well as a necessary change of the registrant's behavior and rectification of register data can lead to **temporary suspension for a period of up to six months or until inaccuracies are corrected, public notification in TR entry**; persistent noncompliance, as unchanged behavior or failure to correct data, leads to a **removal for one year, public notification in the TR, and the withdrawal of access passes**; serious, deliberate noncompliance can result in a **removal for two years, public notification, and access cards to be returned**	Failure of meeting LDA requirements can lead to a notification by the SOS and the CHR; if notification does not lead to an appropriate response within 60 days, the US Attorney for the District of Columbia will further be informed; civil fine up to $200,000, with a maximum of five years of imprisonment

	Generally 10 working days of responding time before suspension; six weeks (56 days in total) before registrant is disbarred	Generally 60 days of responding time before US Attorney is notified
Accessibility of data	Entries fully available; details of contact persons designated for register's operation are hidden	Only very basic information available, complete information requires downloading the whole database
Availability of data about current number of registrants	Every three weeks	SOS: Most current tally available as of September 2012; CHR: instantaneous figures, most current tally considered for this book as of July 2013
Search engine	Register search at TR website	LD-1/LD-2 database, LD-203 database at SOS website; LD-1/LD-2 database, LD-203 database at CHR website
	Entries might not be found due to spelling mistakes, abbreviations, punctuation marks	Entries might not be found due to spelling mistakes, abbreviations, punctuation marks
Maintenance of data	Five years saved in nonpublic part after deactivation	Registration and reports saved for six years
Exit of register	Not covered by IIA	If registrant is no longer employed/retained to carry out lobbying activities; SOS and CHR to be notified; removal of lobbyist's name from every report filed for registrant's clients
Number of registrants	5,844 registrants; with a population of 505 million 86,413.4 EU inhabitants represented per registered lobbying entity	4,744 registrants; with a population of 316[496] million 66,610.5 US inhabitants represented per registered lobbying entity
Guidance	JTRS Guidance; no frequency defined	LDA Guidance; semiannually

Based on the information provided in the Table 4, the research question **"In which facets both registers differ and resemble each other"** can be answered as follows. Whereas lobbying regulation in the United States is rather traditional, historically conditioned, and still maintains the basic right of 1791 for citizens to petition their government, lobbying in the EU can also be traced

---

[496] United States Census Bureau. (2013). U.S. and World Population Clock. http://www.census.gov/popclock/, visited on August 5, 2013.

back to the Union's origin. However, due to the EU's relatively young history and its heterogeneous composition of 28 Member States, lobbying regulations are still internally diverging and under revision at the EU level. Whereas the US register is based on the LDA as amended by HLOGA and can, due to its legal basis, be linked to legal sanctions, the TR was established through a nonlegal interinstitutional agreement not having the power to oblige lobbyists to register.

The fact that the access to both registers is free of charge and possible online is a signal for the intention to make them accessible to the broadest possible audience. A comparison of the particular target groups for registration reveals that they largely resemble each other with the only difference that lobbying entities covered by the TR are subdivided into subcategories due to different disclosure requirements. However, whereas clients in the United States are not obliged by law to register or report, the JTRS expects clients of TR registrants to submit their own registration and declarations. By that, the JTRS does not exclude double counting on purpose and tries to indirectly create a reason for clients to join the TR. At first sight, target groups for application also seem alike since they both include citizens, public officials and personnel, as well as organizations. Taking a closer look, the primary purpose of the TR is to inform EP staff about the background of lobbyists addressing the institution, whereas in the United States the disclosure tool has been designed for citizens' awareness of lobbying activities directed at the Congress and for increasing public trust in the responsible dialogue between the government and interest representatives.

Compared to the IIA, which specifies entities excluded from the scope of registration, the LDA limits the list of entities obliged to register and report by monetary and temporal thresholds. Even if the IIA's list of organizations exempted from registration is to a certain degree detailed and understandable, the EU's heterogeneity and diverging national concepts of legally defining the entities excluded might be an argument for incorporating a threshold into the IIA as well. By that, the target group for registration could be specified more precisely and universally. This is equally important with regard to the particular definitions of 'lobbyists': While the IIA sticks to a rather broad definition, namely the engagement in activities "with the objective of influencing the decision-making processes," the LDA as amended refers to temporal thresholds (more than one contact, 20 percent of time, within a three-month period). Therefore, the definition by the EU might grant too much room for (mis)interpretation.

In terms of preventing the latter through clear and numerous definitions, the LDA seems generally more comprehensive, since in addition to defining lobbyists and their activities, it specifies numerous other entities. This might be a result of the long US tradition and history of lobbying regulation, which has been revised and redefined multiple times, and by which US legislators gathered a whole set of definitions necessary to implement legislation as effectively as possible. Focusing on the US definition, it becomes obvious that 'lobbying activities' here cannot be sufficiently defined without considering the specifications of a 'lobbying contact,' determining that the latter can be established through any oral, written, or electronic communication influencing the (re)formulation or implication of legislation or politics. As a matter of principle, definitions of the LDA are more precise with regard to the target of influence, whereas the IIA provides more details on channels and forms of lobbying contacts and communication.

Contact information filed in the TR is limited to data about the registrant and its employees. By comparison, in the United States, contact data need to inform about the registrant, clients, and entities contributing to or involved in the registrant's activities, and entities holding a share in the client. Again, the US legislation includes a monetary threshold. These differences can be explained by the inherent concept of US politics to allow for massive funding of political campaigning. Conversely, this is not practiced at the EU level; therefore, disclosure of such information is simply unnecessary with regard to the TR. The requirements for the provision of activity-related information also diverge: Whereas EU lobbyists have to submit the number of persons involved in lobbying activities and are just required to name those holding an access pass, the LDA constitutes to name lobbying employees and additionally list their previous positions as executive or legislative officials. Consequently, the US register does not only personalize lobbyists to a higher degree, but further allows for gaining an overview about previous services and, thus, about which potential networks such individuals might still be able to reactivate.

Whereas EU lobbyists are expected to file their general goals and legislative fields of interest, US registrants are determined to name political institutions that they addressed, list the legislative subject of their conversation, and a list of bill numbers of their concern. Even if a 'legislative footprint' is also currently debated in the EU, the LDA again goes far beyond what the IIA could demand—however, in this context, the EU might simply lack the legal basis to impose equal requirements. US registrants are not only obliged to include a statement on having addressed the House of Congress and Federal agencies.

In addition, they need to list all institutions related to the Congress or Federal agencies that have been approached. Therefore, this can be described as two-level contact disclosure. Even if the IIA does not expect registrants to provide as much information about clients as the LDA does, EU legislators are more interested in gaining information about registrants' affiliations to networks. This reflects the characteristic of lobbying in the EU, where interest representation vis-à-vis institutions is frequently proceeded via national or international associations.

Both registers are designed to provide users with the client-related turnover (EU) or the gross income (United States) of lobbying firms, and an estimate about lobbying-related expenses by entities lobbying on their own behalf. With regard to financial disclosure, reporting requirements of both registers vary depending on the legal constitution of the registrant. In contrast to the TR-inherent obligation to list sources and amounts of EU funding, in the United States obligations are designed vice versa. Unsurprisingly, the practice of massive financing of political campaigning has resulted in the regulation to report information about funds contributed to political and governmental entities. Diverging updating requirements reflect once more the limited regulatory possibilities of the EU due to the nonlegal constitution of the IIA. Whereas the agreement only cements that data shall be renewed once a year, registration and reporting under the LDA are not only bound to deadlines by a certain amount of days, but reports are furthermore due to be submitted on a month-related basis.

It is the TR's voluntary approach that links registration to privileges—in the United States, such measures are simply not needed. Whereas the EP and the European Commission have bundled their powers to operate the TR through the JTRS, the United States lacks a single agency operating lobbying disclosure and an agency responsible for enforcement to remedy the fact that the SOS and CHR are not authorized to investigate breaches of law. Whereas the JTRS is restricted in its responsibility of registration revision to random checks, GAO only audits a random sample of registrations and reports annually. As a consequence, neither register can guarantee full accuracy of all registrations and reports filed.

In the context of debating the particular registration requirements it is not surprising that only 47 percent of TR entries checked (March–September 2012) were compliant, whereas the latest GAO report stated that 85 percent of the reports were filed as required and 90 percent of new registrants submitted their reports as expected. This image is further completed by 70 percent among TR registrants that faced difficulties in providing requested information, compared to a majority among US registrants who assessed LD-2 reporting as 'very easy' or 'somewhat easy.' Therefore, it does not seem understandable why a fixed frequency for updating JTRS guidance is not defined by the IIA, although LDA guidance is determined to be renewed semiannually. Due to its legal basis, failure to comply with the regulations of the US register may lead to a civil fine of up to $200,000 or imprisonment of up to five years. The maximum penalty linked to the TR is a removal from the register for two years as well as the obligatory return of the EP access pass. Irrespective of the fact that an interinstitutional agreement does not have the legislative power to justify sanctions, removing interest representatives from the register might be counterproductive to the transparent approach of the TR, even if potentially causing reputational damage to the registrant.

With regard to the accessibility of data, it is a major deficit of the US register that research with both databases on the websites of the SOS and the CHR results in findings that remain at a very basic level; to gain full access, users are forced to download the whole database. Even if this might only be a minor technical effort, accessibility of data is still dependent on technical compatibility of the user's programs. As a consequence, availability of data might be limited. In contrast to that, TR entries are fully available and—if search is successful and boxes were filled properly—can provide users with a helpful tool of background information about the lobbying entity concerned. Whereas the JTRS publishes latest amounts of registrants every three weeks, figures are not provided universally in the United States: In comparison to the CHR that provides instantaneous figures, such as of July 3, 2013, the SOS refers to its recent numbers as of September 2012. This does not only lead to confusion of database users, but might to a certain extent reduce the seriousness of this governmental tool.

As search requests in both the US and EU registers might not lead to any match due to spelling mistakes, mis-spelled abbreviations, or wrong punctuation marks, this can be identified as a common deficit of both systems. Even if the LDA does not oblige registrants to officially report their termination of lobbying activities and notify the SOS and the CHR, the law at least allows for the opportunity. At the other side of the Atlantic, this is not even a voluntary option since the IIA does not consider a termination at all: This might lead to the wrong assumption that a certain entity is still actively engaged in lobbying activities. Finally, a simple calculation shows that statistically, lobbyists in the EU are even more vocal and representative since one registered entity in the TR statistically lobbies on behalf of 86,413.4 EU citizens compared with one US registrant lobbying for 66,610.5 citizens of the United States Due to the fact that the TR was launched only in 2011, numbers of registrants have been continuously rising since its day of implementation. In contrast, the amount of registrants under the LDA remained relatively stable since the act's implementation. Of the general deviations of up to 2,000 lobbyists, none can clearly be ascribed to the implementation of HLOGA in 2007. One can either infer from this result that the amount of lobbyists addressing the US government has generally been relatively stable, or assume that it has always been the same percentage of US lobbyists that considered the LDA as serious lobbying regulation and, thus, decided to register and report.

4.2 Discussion

The following discussion refers to the research questions: **"How do relevant actors and addressees of influence assess the EU register?"**; **"How efficient is the EU's TR in comparison to lobbying registration in the United States?"**; and **"Accordingly, should the EU register become mandatory?"**

⊃ **Incentives for registration: The advantage-focused perspective**

The EP and the European Commission link registration in the TR with several advantages. However, stakeholders and scholars perceive them differently. The public consultation of the JTRS resulted in 76 percent of respondents choosing alerts on public consultations and 69 percent naming alerts on roadmaps as a reason for registration. However, this service necessitates evaluation from two different angles: Whereas the euRobotics Employee as a representative of a newly founded Euro-association assesses the alert mechanism as a helpful advantage,[497] some interviewees are convinced that one has to keep track of public consultations and roadmaps anyway, if a legislative issue is crucial for the particular lobbying entity.[498] BM even categorizes the alerting e-mails as 'spam': They are not perceived as useful since the European Commission would send them only after the particular public consultation has been already announced online and to the media. As the BDI Employee emphasizes, neither the alert mechanism nor the access pass were a main criteria for the

---

[497] euRobotics Employee. (2013). Interview of June 19, 2013.
[498] See BDI Employee (2013).

BDI's registration, but an 'added-value.' It was rather a key intention of the association to present itself through registration as a supporter of transparency.[499] As the BDI's umbrella association, BUSINESSEUROPE would also have registered without the incentivizing badge or the alerting service. Still, badges are considered as 'a second reason' for enrolling.[500] The In-House Lobbyist reflects the view of the euRobotics Employee by assuming that especially smaller companies or associations are the primary beneficiaries of this service.[501]

As further disclosed by the public consultation of the JTRS, 66 percent of respondents considered access badges as a reason for joining the TR.[502] Interestingly, the US Watchdog Representative regards the distribution of badges as a "counterproductive" approach since simplifying access for lobbyists to MEPs could enhance bribery; the CHR Employee also agrees on that.[503] On the contrary, for the DLR Employee, the euRobotics Employee, the WWF Employee, and the In-House Lobbyist access cards are an advantage when entering parliamentary premises.[504] The DLR Employee is also concerned that bribery could be fostered especially if such access badges were *not* distributed.[505] Beyond this, it must be kept in mind that such passes are not the only device for gaining access to the EP—stakeholders can still enter its facilities through personal contacts with MEPs and their staff,[506] or encounter delegates elsewhere.

For the In-house Lobbyist, a general allegation that any lobbyist is potentially corrupt is an indicator for an 'ideological narrow-mindedness' on the comprehension of political participation.[507] This point is also shared by the BDI Employee, who classifies the US Watchdog Representative's approach as 'relatively crude' and an 'awkward comprehension of democracy'—especially from an American perspective.[508] Regardless of categorizing access passes as advantageous, the In-House Lobbyist would change the entrance procedure as

---

[499] BDI Employee (2013).
[500] BUSINESSEUROPE Employee (Interview 2013).
[501] In-house Lobbyist (2013).
[502] JTRS (2012b), p. 12.
[503] US Watchdog Representative (2013a); CHR Employee (2013).
[504] DLR Employee (2013); WWF Employee (2013); In-House Lobbyist (2013); euRobotics Employee (2013).
[505] DLR Employee (2013).
[506] See also Šefčovič (2011), p. 201; the BM Consultant (2013).
[507] In-House Lobbyist (2013).
[508] BDI Employee (2013).

such, since access card holders are required to activate their pass whenever entering the Parliament.[509]

As the BDI Employee adds, reception points need to be sufficiently manned to allow for an 'adequate access.'[510] Another aspect directly linked to incentives of the TR is the potential effect of peer pressure among stakeholders to register. The Commission Representative and the DLR Employee, for instance, are convinced that to a certain degree such group pressure occurs; the DLR Employee's conviction of the idea behind the register has even resulted in an attempt to motivate other colleagues to join.[511] According to the WWF Employee's perception, peer pressure could help to prevent registrants that "fall far off the rules." Still, he regards this rather relevant for "big name consultancies."[512] Apart from such pressure, the In-House Lobbyist even deems it part of the current 'etiquette' to accept the code of conduct by registration.[513] As the euRobotics Employee explains, the current amount of registrants was no pressure for his association to register, even if the latter is totally new to the Brussels terrain.[514] To the BUSINESSEUROPE Employee, there is no peer pressure existent at all—being registered is simply essential since nowadays nobody could 'oppose transparency.'[515]

It is one of the future objectives of the JTRS to increase the current number of TR registrants by extending its incentives.[516] To serve this end, among others Gentili suggests that personnel of both the Commission and the EP should abandon encountering unregistered lobbyists.[517] This demand is also reflected in the annual report of the JTRS: Thus, registrants are to a major degree concerned about the fact that nonregistrants are still not treated equally by EU institutions.[518] Beyond that, ALTER-EU's report of 2013 argues that the refusal of meetings with nonregistrants could even make "registration de facto mandatory."[519] Another approach to create a more incentivized register suggests

---

[509] In-House Lobbyist (2013).
[510] BDI Employee (2013).
[511] DLR Employee (2013); Commission Representative (2013a).
[512] WWF Employee (2013).
[513] In-House Lobbyist (2013).
[514] euRobotics Employee (2013).
[515] BUSINESSEUROPE Employee (2013).
[516] JTRS (2012b), p. 14, 3.1.2.
[517] Gentili (2013), p. V.
[518] JTRS (2012b), p. 13, 2.3.
[519] ALTER-EU (2013), p. 25.

granting the privilege of facilitated access to Commission and Council premises. The In-House Lobbyist favors the option to extend the validity of access passes to the Commission, especially with regard to a more unitary entrance system for Brussels.[520] With respect to a comprehensive register and the TR as a useful tool, the BDI also deems this idea reasonable.[521]

Conversely, the BM Consultant does not see any benefit in expanding accessibility to the Commission. In contrast to the EP, whose facilities need to be entered by badge holders to attend committee sittings or other events, meetings with the Commission are of a direct nature only.[522] Although, for the DLR Employee, the extension of access badges to the Commission is a helpful tool in view of attracting more entities to register, he also identifies the Council of the EU as an important addressee for lobbyists. By interacting with COREPER or national ministers, interest representatives have the opportunity to consult the Council about specific content and offer their expert knowledge in return. Accordingly, he deems it reasonable that the Council joins the Commission and the EP as the third official operator of the TR.[523] In addition, the WWF Employee also names the Council's technical expert groups as targets to circulate expert knowledge.[524] Conversely, the In-House Lobbyist identifies the Council Secretariat as a body that addresses intergovernmental issues and is, therefore, rarely influenced from outside. To him, it is not reasonable if the Council becomes the TR's third official operator.[525] Also the BM Consultant and the BUSINESSEUROPE Employee back this position.[526]

The Council Official also does not favor his institution to become another operator of the TR, since the Council's members are "already subject to their own national transparency rules."[527] Finally, the MEP has the impression that some Council representatives are simply not lobbied in Brussels, but in their particular capital cities. Hence, some Member States are assumed to fear that the TR might 'spill over' to their capital cities.[528] The BUSINESSEUROPE Employee

---

[520] In-House Lobbyist (2013).
[521] BDI Employee (2013).
[522] The BM Consultant (2013).
[523] DLR Employee (2013).
[524] WWF Employee (2013).
[525] In-House Lobbyist (2013).
[526] The BM Consultant (2013); BUSINESSEUROPE Employee (2013).
[527] Official of the Council. (2013b). E-mail received July 9, 2013.
[528] The MEP (2013).

judges the overall incentivizing of the TR as sufficient,[529] whereas Gentili concludes the exact opposite.[530] Finally, the BM Consultant also explains that to BM incentives for registration are "virtually not existent."[531]

⊃ Incentives for registration: The reputational perspective

As JTRS figures show, the main motivation of voluntary registrants is to demonstrate transparency in their cooperation with EU institutions (92 percent) and by that to "reflect positively on their image" (93 percent).[532] Among the politicians that were surveyed by BM, 64 percent named the transparency of a lobbyist as a decisive factor for their decision to talk to such a person; 57 percent made the public registration of interest representatives a criterion.[533] The BDI describes transparency as a 'very sensitive topic' for lobbyists and an issue that the BDI decided to address offensively. To serve this end, the association has established its own working group on the TR to discuss the register and promote an offensive strategy of transparency among its 38 member associations.[534]

With regard to the BDI's umbrella association BUSINESSEUROPE, the BUSINESSEUROPE Employee explains that all its members (that are individual legal entities) are encouraged to file their own registration in addition to the registration of the association.[535] Also BM approaches registration from the reputational angle, as the BM Consultant underlines: "it's better to be seen in [the register] and to be a leader in terms of the conduct of transparent lobbying." Therefore, BM tried to set standards of quality responses, such as by listing websites of their clients in its registration entry.[536] As a means to make its registration visible also during daily business contacts, the consultancy has decided to include its own registration number into its e-mail signature, for instance. This is also a means applied by the WWF, whose registration number is an element of its official letterhead.[537] The Commission Representative concedes to the TR the possibility of altering the public perception of lobbyists;[538]

---

[529] BUSINESSEUROPE Employee (2013).
[530] Gentili (2013), p. 14.
[531] The BM Consultant (2013).
[532] JTRS (2012b), 2.2.
[533] Burson Marsteller (2013), p. 67.
[534] BDI Employee (2013).
[535] BUSINESSEUROPE Employee (2013).
[536] The BM Consultant (2013).
[537] WWF Employee (2013).
[538] Commission Representative (2013a).

also, the In-House Lobbyist points out that it could be a means to underline their commitment to play by the rules and express their social responsibility.[539]

◯ **Overall perception of the register**
Assessing the TR's effectiveness and efficiency requires analyzing the general perception of the register. Pointing to the TR's current amount of 5,844 registrants, the Commission Representative assures that to the Commission this number means "quite a good result."[540] Also the BDI Employee concludes that numerous entities already registered, and opines that the industry takes the TR seriously. Since the concept works 'incredibly well' as a bottom-line, the implementation of a mandatory concept in the EU is unnecessary.[541] In addition to the MEP, who classifies the register as a good step forward,[542] the JTRS Staff is convinced that also registrants would agree that the TR improved and "stimulated a lot of academic research."[543] Since the TR increased the debate about transparency in general, the BM Consultant identifies its pure existence as the greatest benefit.[544] The BDI describes the TR as a possibility to win and enforce acceptance for competitive democracy.[545] Also BUSINESSEUROPE is well aware of the extreme importance of transparency. According to the BUSINESSEUROPE Employee, "the utmost important currency of lobbyists is trust and professionalism." However, with regard to some NGOs and antilobby campaigning, he warns not to degenerate the TR into a "witch hunt."[546] One of the groups he might refer to is ALTER-EU, which in its report of 2013 deems the TR's voluntary approach to be "neither realistic nor sustainable" to secure transparency.[547] In a broader context of such criticism, the BDI Employee points out that lobby watchdogs and campaigners lack facts about registration on which they could actually base their criticism—thus, they present 'crudely distorted facts' or unrealistic demands.[548] However, Ahrens argues that lobbying regulation is unable to render the opaque field of mass actors at EU level into a more transparent and structured one—a register could at best be one

---

[539] In-house Lobbyist (2013).
[540] Commission Representative (2013a).
[541] BDI Employee (2013).
[542] The MEP (2013).
[543] JTRS Staff (2013a).
[544] The BM Consultant (2013).
[545] BDI Employee (2013).
[546] BUSINESSEUROPE Employee (2013).
[547] ALTER-EU (2013), p. 24.
[548] BDI Employee (2013).

step into the right direction and a starting point for a general comprehensive reform.[549]

⊃ **The complexity of registration requirements**

Specifications about expected information to be filed in the TR should be understandable and precise; some of them leave room for interpretation and dissatisfy registrants. Despite the fact that 77 percent of interviewees of the public consultation identified reporting guidelines as "clear" or "very clear,"[550] there is an overall demand among interest representatives and TR critics for clarified information about the general definition of lobbying, estimates of scope-related personnel, and the disclosure of financial data.[551] The latter is particularly a concern of the BM Consultant, since the corporate category of registrants uses "vastly different approaches" to estimate its finances. In contrast to information about a lobbying entity and its legislative interest, he does not regard financial disclosure necessarily helpful.[552] The In-House Lobbyist suggests that the JTRS redefines data disclosure about EU funding, since such grants are often used to support projects that involve several entities at once. Thus, breaking down the different extents of involvement is sometimes difficult to realize.[553] However, the register should be kept as simple as possible to avoid the disclosure of complex data that could potentially infringe on accounting rules.[554] To serve all these demands, the JTRS has announced in its annual report of 2012 to provide further guidance and definitions on "eligible activities and expenditures."[555] Another aspect evoking criticism by the BM Consultant is the TR's continuous lack of a clear definition of lobbyists in general.

The annual report of the JTRS points out that consultancies obviously prefer reporting conditions to be equalized, especially considering law firms that are "still widely absent from the TR."[556] However, the JTRS considers proposing to participants of the TR's revision to "envisage an ad-hoc, derogative and exceptional formula for category I entities claiming a need for client confidentiality, subject to the demonstration of concrete and non-hypothetical risks associated

---

[549] Ahrens ([1]2007), pp. 142f.
[550] JTRS (2012b), p. 13
[551] For example, see BUSINESSEUROPE Employee (2013).
[552] The BM Consultant (2013).
[553] See In-House Lobbyist (2013).
[554] Ibid.
[555] JTRS (2012b), p. 14, 3.1.2.
[556] JTRS (2012b), p. 13.

with the divulgation of these."[557] Whereas ALTER-EU warns that this exception could undermine "the very purpose of the register,"[558] the In-House Lobbyist argues that it is a general right of the public to gain insight into the activities of agencies that accept third-party contracts to advertise targets other than their own. Therefore, clients of such agencies should be disclosed.[559] As emphasized by the BM Consultant, there is no reason for law firms to hide behind the demand of their Bar Association to stick to client confidentiality, unless a client in trial pays these firms for legal advice. According to Thomas M. Susman, Director of Governmental Affairs at the American Bar Association, at the "OECD Forum on Transparency and Integrity in Lobbying,"[560] he did not understand the abstention of lawyers from the EU register: In the United States, however, registration had never been a problem for this group.[561]

A Senior Consultant of a nonregistered Brussels-based consulting business explains why registration is hardly possible for her company: By its contracts, the consultancy agrees with its clients not to disclose any information about them, which also includes not listing their names in a lobbying register. Therefore, registration would require getting the permission of every single client to be named. Compared with trade representatives, for law or consulting firms this effort would be disproportional. A mandatory register would force the consultancy to restructure its contracts and adapt to the disclosure of clients.[562] However, a recent OECD study has revealed that around 55 percent of the interviewed lobbyists support the disclosure of clients' names.[563]

➔ **Monitoring the register**

The surveillance of the TR is a particularly highly debated matter. As outlined in Chapter 3.1.3, obviously the JTRS 'relies' to a certain extent on watchdog organizations and the public to monitor the register, such as through alerting or complaining tools. ALTER-EU confirms that indeed in the past it felt 'hinted at' by the European Commission to take over a part of this responsibility.[564]

---

[557] Ibid. p. 14, 3.2.
[558] ALTER-EU (2013), p. 23.
[559] In-house lobbyist (2013).
[560] The BM Consultant (Interview 2013).
[561] Ibid.
[562] Senior Consultant of a Nonregistered Brussels-based Consultancy. (2012). Telephone interview of June 12, 2013.
[563] OECD. (2010b). Transparency and Integrity in Lobbying. http://ec.europa.eu/enlargement/taiex/dyn/create_speech.jsp?speechID=16281&key=c39c5ed4225bb66e3049c5ad72f54783, visited on January 16, 2013.
[564] EU Watchdog Representative. (2013c). E-mail received on May 21, 2013.

This is contrary to the In-House Lobbyist's opinion that ALTER-EU's responsibility for this practice would be inappropriate, since the JTRS should be able to realize this duty on its own. Regardless of the fact that ALTER-EU is not mandated to participate in the monitoring process, it is always 'dangerous' to declare as guardians those entities that appoint themselves as watchdogs. As he warns, this could cause ideological narrow-mindedness and might even jeopardize the register's reputation.[565] According to the BUSINESSEUROPE Employee, organizations contribute to monitoring since they regard this as part of their mission. However, he does not agree on the assumption that the JTRS has 'sourced out' parts of its controlling duty.[566]

The Commission Representative and the BDI Employee categorize the current number of JTRS Staff as 'sufficient'[567]; the BDI Employee even adds that an excessive number of personnel is unnecessary here since the Secretariat is already 'highly skilled' for its tasks.[568] The MEP questions whether additional means of controlling would be effective at all since extending capacities is also a question of increasing bureaucracy.[569] Likewise, the In-House Lobbyist agrees that one should weigh the possibility to stick to random but intensive checks and the option to implement more complex procedures that require additional staff.[570] However, one of ALTER-EU's main diagnoses about the TR is that the JTRS is currently "understaffed": The organization expects more institutional commitment by deploying more monitoring staff.[571]

◎ **Perception of a mandatory approach**

An aspect of the TR, which evokes probably the most extensive discussion, is the question whether registration should become obligatory or not. Even if the Commission presents the TR as "*de facto* mandatory," the Commission Representative admits that the register's obligatoriness is "as de facto as possible."[572] In fact, the decision to conclude an IIA to establish the TR enhanced the call for a mandatory system and essential steps to prepare "for a transition to mandatory registration" during the revision process.[573] As the Commission

---

[565] In-House Lobbyist (2013).
[566] BUSINESSEUROPE Employee (2013).
[567] Commission Representative. (2013c). E-mail received on May 7, 2013.
[568] BDI Employee (2013).
[569] The MEP (2013).
[570] In-House Lobbyist (2013).
[571] EU Watchdog Representative (2013a).
[572] Commission Representative (2013a).
[573] European Parliament (2011).

Representative accentuates, the TR could become mandatory if the Treaties provided a legal basis and Member States politically agreed on it. However, at the moment he does not see this opportunity.[574] Beyond that, he ascribes to numerous mandatory systems the phenomenon that numbers of registered lobbyists remain rather low.[575] ALTER-EU even considers a mandatory system "the only sustainable way to secure transparency" around interest representatives.[576] Also the US Watchdog Representative supports a compulsory approach, suggesting that the EU should orientate its registration system on the US system, learn from its shortcomings, and create a better and mandatory register.

To him, a mandatory system is the only adequate approach: "A lobbyist registry must be mandatory, in order to be accurate and fair. If it is not mandatory, only those who have nothing to hide will register."[577] A survey among lobbyists based in the United States and Brussels, which was conducted in 2008, revealed that 25.7 percent backed voluntary registration, opposed to 66.2 percent that favored a mandatory system.[578] In addition, a BM survey of 2013 that addressed Brussels-based policy makers even resulted in 79 percent in favor of a mandatory system, of which 48 percent expected it to be implemented within the next three years[579]. However, it should be kept in mind that the consultancy itself—as the publisher of the study—explicitly encourages the idea of a compulsory system. The BM Consultant as its representative regards a mandatory approach advantageous, since guidelines are specified to a major degree.[580]

On the contrary, the DLR Employee compares obligatory registration to a "threat with a cudgel."[581] Even if the EP officially favors a compulsory system,[582] the MEP is convinced that an obligation to register will not be on debate before 2018, but might include sanctions for those who consciously and deliberately

---

[574] Commission Representative (2013).
[575] Commission Representative. (2013d). Comment made during live debate "Mandatory or Voluntary? Time for a Register that Really Works!", European Parliament. June 17, 2013.
[576] ALTER-EU (2013), p. 25.
[577] US Watchdog Representative (2013a).
[578] Holman and Luneburg (2012).
[579] Burson Marsteller (2013), p. 22.
[580] The BM Consultant (2013).
[581] DLR Employee (2013).
[582] Macovei, M. (MEP). (2013). Represented through her assistant during live debate "Mandatory or Voluntary? Time for a Register that Really Works!", European Parliament. June 17, 2013.

submit wrong information and break the code of conduct.[583] In representing the view of MEPs, he notes that total surveillance of delegates who hold a free mandate is simply impossible—unless by video footage.[584] And as the IIA underlines, the TR should still allow MEPs to maintain their respected right to "exercise their parliamentary mandate without restriction."[585] The BDI assesses a compulsory system neither as efficacious, nor as an impulse to change the current state of Brussels lobbying to a major degree. An obligation to register might only 'pillory' industry in the public debate. From the perception of the BDI Employee, the request for a mandatory system implies once again the cliché of lobbying to take place behind closed doors.[586] The In-House Lobbyist identifies the voluntary supply of information in particular as a great strength of democracy.[587]

Beyond that, the JTRS Staff hints at another interesting aspect: Since the current design of the TR welcomes 'all types of organizations,' a mandatory system may require a reduction of this range. Therefore, it would be a more practical approach to make it 'step by step' unavoidable for interest representatives to stay out of the register.[588] Even if the EU Lobbying Expert is convinced that a mandatory register might bring more stakeholders "above surface," to him it is a major disadvantage that an obligatory system always requires a "detailed legal text that lawyers can always challenge" since this might cause a lot of litigation. As a strength of the voluntary approach, he points to the motivation for special NGOs and media to check registration of lobbyists and publish their results.[589] Instead of launching compulsory registration, the Council Official prefers that the current system be applied correctly.[590] The WWF Employee expects a change in the TR's constitution toward a mandatory system to be linked with the "maturing of EU institutions," which he estimates to first show results in 2020. By that, registry would become inevitable.[591]

As it is often claimed, the EU should let itself be influenced by the mandatory registration system of the United States. In its report of 2013, ALTER-EU even

---

[583] The MEP (2013).
[584] Ibid.
[585] Official Journal of the European Union (2011), I.(4).
[586] BDI Employee (2013).
[587] In-House Lobbyist (2013).
[588] JTRS Staff (2013a).
[589] EU Lobbying Expert (2013).
[590] Council Official (2013).
[591] WWF Employee (2013).

expects the TR "not only to catch up, but to over-take" the US registration system.[592] However, Woll warns that before the US model can be partially replicated in the EU, it is essential to examine the applicability of the US American concept with regard to the EU's public policy process, its institutions, and the inherent variety of national political systems.[593] Even if the Commission started examining the US register for some possible "inspiration," personally the Commission Representative does not consider the US register as a model one could entirely copy in the EU.[594] In addition, from the US Watchdog Representative's perspective the TR has still "a way to go" before he would recommend to copy parts of the North American system.[595] Finally, Commissioner Šefčovič also presented himself as rather hesitant about a full adaption of the US system: "[…] while many people describe the US federal lobbyist registration system as more efficient because it is mandatory and equipped with penal sanctions, the reality of its operation seems to be more nuanced" due to deficits of formal enforcement measures.[596]

○ Sanctions

It is not only TR-related sanctions that cause controversy, but also penalties imposed by the US government for disobedience to registration laws. Considering the possibility of a temporary or permanent removal of registrants from the TR, the US Watchdog Representative contradicts this approach by stating that it defeats "the point of the register" to create transparent decision-making and serve the fundamental democratic right to lobby.[597] With regard to public notifications in the TR about registrants that have broken the code of conduct, the In-House Lobbyist is convinced that this can have "a certain effect" on registrants' behavior, namely, to avoid further notifications in their entry.[598] The BM Consultant is less optimistic about the current sanctioning measures of the TR and deems them to be "pretty weak"; even if they certainly had some impact on consultancies, there would be hardly any for large cooperations. If TR sanctions were to be changed, he would suggest the changes to be monetary.[599]

---

[592] ALTER-EU (2013), p. 19.
[593] Friedrich (2010), p. 45.
[594] Commission Representative (2013a).
[595] US Watchdog Representative (2013a).
[596] Šefčovič (2013).
[597] US Watchdog Representative (2013).
[598] In-House Lobbyist (2013).
[599] The BM Consultant (2013).

The WWF Employee also agrees that some types of financial and even penal sanctions would be necessary, and could be designed similarly to those in the United States.[600] Conversely, the MEP underlines that imposing the same sanctions as in the United States would be a few 'bar-bells too much to lift' for the EU system.[601] Irrespectively, as of the current state of knowledge of the CHR Employee, the penalty of imprisonment has yet not been imposed in the United States.[602] The BUSINESSEUROPE Employee does not even see the possibility to impose such sanctions in the EU.[603] Meanwhile, the BDI Employee considers the whole debate about possibly linking a mandatory TR to sanctions unneeded and as an inappropriate treatment with interest representatives in general.[604] Finally, the EU Lobbying Expert points out that social control of the TR is more effective than legal control since it "penalises groups below surface" through public scandalizing.[605]

---

[600] WWF Employee (2013).
[601] The MEP (2013).
[602] CHR Employee (2013).
[603] BUSINESSEUROPE Employee (2013).
[604] BDI Employee (2013).
[605] EU Lobbying Expert (2013).

↪ Discussion overview

Table 5.[606] Discussion overview

Table 5 presents answers of actors and experts to key questions related to the improvement of the TR.

✓: yes; x: no; T: Tendency; -: not part of interview.

Interviewee	Mandatory (M)/Voluntary (V)?	Extending validity of access passes to Commission	Council to become the third official TR operator	Pass perceived as advantageous	Alert mechanism perceived as advantageous
JTRS Staff	T: V	-	-	-	-
Commission Representative	T: V	X	✓	✓	✓
MEP[607]	M	-	T: X	✓	-
Council Official[608]	V	X	X	✓	✓
EU Watchdog Representative (ALTER-EU)	M	-	✓	✓	✓
In-House Lobbyist	V	✓	X	✓	✓
EU Lobbying Expert	V	-	-	-	-
WWF Employee	M	✓	✓	✓	✓
DLR Employee[609]	V	✓	✓	✓	✓
BM Consultant	M	X	✓	✓	X
BUSINESS EUROPE Employee	V	T: X	✓	✓	✓

---

[606] euRobotics has been left out of consideration since the European association was simply too new in Brussels to have enough background knowledge for an appropriate judgment.
[607] Official view of the EP, not of the MEP.
[608] Council Official (2013b).
[609] Personal view of the DLR Employee, not an official view of the DLR.

⊃ **"How do relevant actors and addressees of influence assess the EU register?"**

Even if respondents to the public consultation expressed that access passes and the Commission's alerting service were incentives for registry, the interviews revealed that both tools were often assessed as a secondary motivation or an added value. Therefore, registration *per se* and demonstrating that one's entity commits itself to a transparent political dialogue can be identified as a primary reason for registration. As research results further demonstrate, advantage-related incentives for joining the TR still have to be amended. However, especially for new registrants or those entities that are new to the political system of Brussels the alerting tool can be categorized as helpful. Interviewees disagree concerning the question whether a certain peer pressure among Brussels-based lobbyists to join the TR exists. Although registration is regarded as part of the etiquette, it may also cause spill-over effects in that it persuades registrants to motivate others to join. It would be a helpful secondary effect if the TR could create such a pressure. However, the motivation to disclose information by this tool seemingly remains limited to personal perceptions of transparency.

As a matter of fact, registration is even applied as a 'counter-argument' to the image of lobbying which several watchdogs convey. This implies that especially for lobbyists, the TR is a pivotal instrument to maintain an appropriate impression of their profession. Analysis also discovers a general agreement that the TR should be further incentivized by granting the privilege to meet with EU institutional staff to registrants only. This demand emphasizes that if registrants are asked to respect the TR as a serious tool, EU institutions should do this as well. The accession of the Council as a third operator is both an option laid down in the IIA and a goal identified by the JTRS, but both remain unachieved.[610] Respondents disagree concerning the possibility that the Council could be responsible for cooperating with the TR. It is a rather common assumption that lobbying activities addressed to the Council mostly take place in the capitals of Member States. The idea that the extension of the validity of access passes to the Commission's premises could create a unified EU entrance system and increase the usefulness and comprehensiveness of the TR stands in opposition to the argumentation that Commission meetings differ from those in the Parliament. Consequently, especially in terms of monitoring

---

[610] Gentili (2013), p. 9.

the current legislative procedure and attending political EP events, such as debates or votes, the Parliament is a more relevant and attractive addressee for interest representatives.

As a matter of principle, its registrants use the TR as a serious instrument to underline their valuation of transparency; this is also demonstrated by entities that include their registration numbers into their contact details. Thus, one could talk about a 'business card of transparency' here. Scholars state that the TR may even motivate listed entities to the attempt of setting standards by quality responses. This can be assessed as evidence that listed stakeholders are ambitious to contribute to the TR's development, also in view of their reputation. Registration specifications could be adapted more to registrants' needs and the feasibility of certain requirements, such as financial estimations or information about EU funding in particular. Furthermore, the EU could operate a register that is shaped in cooperation with lobbyists and not merely imposed on them—this would be a mutual benefit. In summary, all interviewees agree that the current concepts and effects of the TR are generally judged as a positive step into a politically more transparent future. Furthermore, the TR is ascribed the power to promote acceptance of complementary democracy. Since the register also inspired academic research, a certain interest to examine the effectiveness and efficiency of the TR is obviously existent among scholars and the public society.

Generally, registration requirements are still criticized for being too complex, demanding they be simplified as soon as possible. Likewise, lobbying under the scope of the TR should be further defined, if the EU intends the TR to become a respected instrument that is sustained in being taken seriously by its target group. Moreover, concretized and narrower definitions as well as specifications are also expected to be less complicated than before. However, earlier the emphatic demand for these amendments demonstrates that for those critics, the TR is an accepted tool. By further clarification, the TR would also adapt to the suggestion of the OECD more appropriately: Pursuant to the organization's experience, a "strong lobbying regulation" should contain "clear and unambiguous" definitions to prevent misinterpretation and close loopholes.[611] As long as current registration requirements are maintained, it is also a good solution to follow the example of the BDI to develop internal guidelines for a consistent interpretation of such requirements.[612]

---

[611] OECD (2010b).
[612] BDI Employee (2013).

By monitoring the TR's registration process, watchdogs are perceived to approach this responsibility as part of their mission. Thus, ALTER-EU feels at times put in charge of the monitoring by the European Commission. Some might argue that the EU has chosen an easy way in that it 'complements' register monitoring by complaints and alerts of watchdogs and the public. Conversely, involving external resources seems rather pivotal in view of the current amount of 5,844 registrants and just four JTRS Staff. Moreover, the concept of social control could even promote the virtue of citizens to strengthen transparency and an open political dialogue of the democratic system they are part of. Interviewees mostly agree that the current status quo of four JTRS Staff executing and handling random quality checks, complaints, and alerts is sufficient, and prefer this situation to an increased bureaucratic effort. In conclusion, the preference to maintain the status quo of monitoring forces is obviously linked to the following assumption: Namely, that an increase in surveillance activities and the number of JTRS Staff again might evoke the image of lobbying as something negative, requiring sound control. On the contrary, ALTER-EU assails the JTRS to be insufficiently staffed.

While to ALTER-EU a mandatory system seems the single solution for the TR, and a majority of respondents to the presented surveys favors an obligation to register, persons interviewed for this study mainly support the opposite approach. As argued, a mandatory TR would not change the general attitude of those entities that generally decide to refuse disclosing their data. Furthermore, the detection of all those who break the law by nonregistration would require tremendous human resources, whereas a voluntary system is based on social control. Moreover, respondents note that obligatory registration could increase litigation, and on the other hand might reduce the scope of organizations and entities covered by the register; this could be a stark loss for transparency in general. As further perceived, the discussion about a mandatory TR implies that lobbying is something rather negatively connoted. This could lead to the supposition that one can infer from the constitution of a certain lobby register how a particular society valuates and treats the profession of lobbyists.

However, compulsory registration can only be implemented in the EU if a legal basis exists. Even if the study of the University of Erlangen-Nürnberg argues that this is the case, it still cannot be considered as given that all 28 Member States would agree on such a system. Beyond that, establishing compulsory registration in the EU is limited to the degree to which MEPs will agree on being indirectly monitored through the TR. Especially the debate about sanctioning measures shows controversies. Whereas some respondents clearly favor a mandatory TR to include sanctions similar to those in the United States, others generally oppose sanctions, consider social control to be more effective—even if sanctions of a mandatory register would not necessarily exclude the latter—and deem the whole debate about penalties to be a wrong and dispensable signal. Overall, one can conclude that a major amount of respondents considers penalties from a reputational perspective.

Subsequently, the question **"How effective and efficient the EU's TR is"** needs to be answered. As a matter of principle, with regard to the accessibility of information about registrants the TR can be described as more efficient than the system in the United States, since simple search immediately reveals the registrant's complete entry and subcategories of registrants allow for a better overview. Additionally, entries detail contact data; therefore, TR users are provided with a source for further information about the registered entity if necessary. By including information about registrants' active involvement in associations or federations, the TR serves the one-stop-shop principle and, thus, makes research more efficient. However, the efficiency is limited due to the fact that entries do not contain information about previously held political posts. Moreover, spelling mistakes may prevent the searched entry from being found and cause confusion for the website user.

It is equally inefficient that the IIA does not provide any information about how to handle termination of lobbyists; therefore, users might again be confused because of missing entries or entries indicating that the entity concerned is still active in lobbying. Although the TR can be perceived as an effective tool in terms of promoting a transparent image of registrants and, thus, supporting their positive reputation, its very broad definition of a 'lobbyist' leaves too much room for (mis)interpretations and might, thus, not cover all lobbying entities under its scope. Consequently, the IIA is ineffective here. Effectiveness is further limited due to a lacking deadline for entry updates—rather broad requirements for annual updating can again be realized differently. In case a common deadline by a certain date proves unfeasible for 28 Member States, at least an automatic notification mechanism should be installed to remind registrants as soon as their update is overdue. Conversely, lobbying activities and channels of communication are precisely specified, and therefore need to be assessed as effective.

Even if to date no specific data about the TR's target group of application are available, responses by interviewees as well as numbers of unique website visitors lead to the assumption that either awareness-raising measures by the

JTRS are not sufficiently effective, or the general acceptance for the TR as a helpful tool is still limited. Since 53 percent of registration entries controlled through quality checks by the JTRS were noncompliant and 70 percent among registrants faced difficulties with registration requirements, specifications and definitions must be considered as ineffective to a certain degree. The effectiveness would increase if TR guidance were published more frequently. Even if it is efficient that the JTRS as the TR's single operator is also the institution in charge of imposing measures on noncompliant registrants, effectiveness is restricted to a major degree due to limited staff resources and inability to guarantee the accuracy of all entries. Access cards and e-mail alerts by the Commission are generally considered as incentives for registration; however, alerts for roadmaps and public consultations are limited in their effectiveness since seemingly most lobbyists follow important legislative issues already on their own. In addition, the effectiveness of access cards is still dependent on the current number of security staff in the EP. That both the effectiveness and efficiency of the TR can still be improved is also demonstrated by the identified approaches for improvement as outlined in Chapter 4.3.

Accordingly, should the EU register become mandatory? Even if a small majority of respondents favors a voluntary approach, registration with the TR should become mandatory. Not because lobbying is necessarily something corrupt or 'bad,' but simply because it forms an essential part of democratic decision-making and should thus be as transparent as possible. As low registrant numbers of law firms and consultancies demonstrate, a voluntary register cannot cover all interest representatives. Even if a mandatory one is not a guarantee to achieve full coverage, a legal obligation as well as a possible sanctioning mechanism is very likely to increase pressure among lobbyists. However, compulsory registration can only be effective if sanctioning is technically feasible.

Irrespective of the fact that a legal basis is still under discussion at the EU level and might require a Treaty change, a mandatory TR can only be implemented with an increased amount of JTRS staff resources. This again depends on the degree to which the EU generally takes lobbying registration seriously. If requirements for financial disclosure in particular were simplified and guidance was provided more often, the bureaucratic effort of registration and updating could be reduced. Moreover, as a matter of principle, mandatory registration in the EU should not reduce the scope of organizations covered, and should maintain the privilege of access passes for registrants and continue to involve the public as an active participant in controlling measures, for instance by complaints and alerts. Before obligatory registration might be realized in the EU, the suggestion to render registration step-wise inevitably would be a good solution in the direction of a '*de facto* mandatory' register. Overall, it still remains the most pivotal step for the EU and its citizens not to approach registration as a requirement imposed on 'bad' and opaque lobbyists as an instrument of control, but as something that is a matter of course. As it seems, the EU has still a long way to go.

4.3 Incentives for improvement

Focusing on the question "**to what extent the effectiveness and efficiency of the EU register can be increased**," the following approaches to improved and more incentivized lobbying registration in the EU can be specified: An interesting aspect that has hardly ever been addressed is the fact that registrants are not bound to using a certain language for submission of their data. Consequently, apart from financial information and contact details, users might simply not be able to understand the information provided.[613] Therefore, TR revision should consider implementing the requirement to **file all data in English**. Taking the example of the United States, it would be reasonable if registrants and their lobbying employees had to **disclose all governmental and political posts previously held at EU level or in Member States** to allow for a comprehensive overview about which networks might still be activated. Further information to be disclosed are registrants' memberships in **MEP-Industry forums**: Even if they are considered as informal groupings that are not officially recognized by the EP and maintained under the "sole responsibility" of MEPs,[614] they should generally be publicly listed in a voluntary register that could be linked to the TR. Such an additional tool could be used to reveal their members, goals, and sources of income. Equally important, TR revision should debate whether it would be a feasible idea to install a kind of **'lobby ticker'** on websites of MEPs and Commissioners, informing website visitors about meetings and events with or organized by interest representatives. This is also already in practice in the White House.

Focusing on the section of consultancies and law firms in particular, additional **incentives** need to become more persuasive as long as the TR remains voluntary. On the one hand, this could be achieved through a **narrower definition**

---

[613] Macovei (2013).
[614] JTRS Staff (e-mail 2013d).

of the term 'lobbyist.' This should also include **temporal thresholds**, such as a certain percentage of working time dedicated to lobbying activities, a certain amount of lobbying contacts and—with particular focus on EU lobbying—it should consider activities linked to national or international associations. On the other hand, the TR can only be incentivized to a higher degree if personnel of the EP as well as of the Commission would be stricter in **meeting only those entities that have joined the TR**—if both institutions expect lobbyists to take the TR seriously, they should do the same. The inclusion of an exceptional formula for professional consultancies, law firms, and self-employed consultants is contra-productive; registrations of consultancies or law firms do not entirely serve the concept of transparency if they do not disclose on behalf of which clients they work. An amended IIA should contain a provision ruling the handling of **termination of lobbying activities**. To prevent confusion, henceforth, registrants should be able to inform the JTRS about their termination and search results should notify users about a registrant's termination of such activities.

With regard to reputational damage, temporary or permanent removal from the TR seems to be an effective solution at first sight. However, this contradicts the idea of creating greater transparency of EU lobbying. A better option might again be the consequence that noncompliant registrants will not be able to meet with EU officials for a certain period. In case the JTRS identifies certain inaccuracies of a registrant's entry and the latter fails to respond in the granted timeframe, **access passes** of all lobbyists employed by the registrant concerned should be **withdrawn for a duration equal to the suspension**. Another aspect related to the accessibility of the EP is a potential restriction of work of larger entities caused by the current limit that only four employees of one single entity are allowed to sojourn in the EP at once. A more appropriate regulation might be linked to a certain **threshold**, as that a certain amount (here: threshold) of access card holders belonging to one single registered organization justifies to grant access to a certain percentage of those group members at once. Even if access passes are granted for one year, in practice, they still have to be 'activated' by security staff every time the cardholder enters the EP. Solutions for a less time-consuming procedure could include **self-service activation terminals**, similar to those in the EP that inform visitors about current sittings and events. Since it would be an additional incentive to **expand the validity of access passes to premises of the Commission** and administrative access procedures could be reduced in time, this option should equally be debated during revision. Even if the Council might be only indirectly lobbied, it remains an important body where political decisions can still come to a halt. Supporting the Commission and the EP as the TR's **third official operator** could, therefore, stimulate acceptance among lobbyists for the register.

If dates of publication for financial year-end reports in the 28 EU Member States allow, for matters of comparability, the JTRS should consider the implementation of a **fixed deadline** for all registrants to update their financial data at the same time. The BM Consultant even suggests setting semiannual deadlines for consultancies and law firms to update their list of clients.[615] Another idea would be to use the alerting e-mail service of the Commission, which could send a **notification** to registrants as soon as their data are due for updating. To simplify financial disclosure, another idea worth considering is to **link** the box where registrants are expected to disclose their source and amount of EU funding to the Commission's newly established **'New Financial Transparency System,'** designed for searching recipients of financial support granted by this institution.[616] By that, registrants would only have to calculate such estimates once.

Generally, **measures of awareness raising** by the JTRS, such as workshops, should be intensified to enhance the role of the TR as an informative tool for more transparent lobbying. To control the degree to which the TR is applied by parliamentary staff, certain **software** could be installed to record only those **unique website visits** coming from IP addresses belonging to the EP. Likewise, the **quantity of quality checks** should be increased, as soon as personnel resources would allow for this. Since a majority of registrants faced difficulties to fulfill disclosure requirements, distinct research among representatives of all six sections of lobbying entities should identify the most common filing mistakes and gather suggestions about how best to prevent them. Complementarily, the IIA should require the JTRS to **publish guidelines on a semiannual basis**.

Concerning the US lobby register, the CHR Employee reflects the suggestion of the Task Force on Federal Lobbying Laws of the American Bar Association to make it an additional obligation under the LDA for registrants to **identify by name the legislative and executive branch officials** they met.[617] As research in the context of this book has collated, scholars and critics share the view that enforcement under the LDA should be undertaken through a **single**

---

[615] The BM Consultant (2013).
[616] See also EU Watchdog Representative (2013a).
[617] CHR Employee (2013); Levin (2011), p. vii.

administrative agency. For an improved system that leads to less confusion and is able to provide users with universal figures, both the SOS and the CHR should install a **common website incorporating one single database** for both types of reports. Search engines of both registration systems in the EU and the United States necessarily require **new programming** to achieve higher tolerance toward misspellings, abbreviations, and punctuation marks. Finally, also under the LDA, clients should be obliged to file their own registrations and reports to allow for an overview of lobbying firms hired to represent their interests.

Regarding the question **"Can the US approach be taken as a reference model for the EU register?"**, the following aspects require being taken into account: Even if research revealed a rather hesitant attitude toward taking registration under the LDA as a model for the EU, especially with regard to the inclusion of certain temporal and monetary thresholds linked to registration requirements, the US register and its underlying legislation can be taken as a reference for narrower definitions. Particularly by thresholds, specifications become applicable to a broad scope of lobbying entities and reduce room for interpretation. Furthermore, the US approach demonstrates how target persons and bodies of lobbying activities should equally be specified more precisely. For a potentially amended IIA, the EU should consider the LDA's inclusion of deadlines for data updates as well as the obligation for registration operators to revise and amend registration guidance on a semiannual basis. To provide TR users with a helpful overview about previous political posts held by employees of registrants and thus to indirectly inform about networks that might still be maintained, the EP and the European Commission should debate about covering this by registration requirements as well. An equal advantage of the US registration scheme is that reports have to inform about termination of lobbying activities by the registrant. This is an option the JTRS should equally consider. Contrarily, TR revision should exclude the option of removing registrants from the TR since it contradicts the concept of transparency by 'removing' lobbyists from a visible surface.

Even if several aspects can serve as a kind of orientation for the TR's design, the applicability of the US approach remains limited, especially with regard to the two different databases showing inconsistent numbers, limited data accessibility due to a limited data storage capacity of governmental websites, a rather low technical tolerance toward spelling mistakes, and the exclusion of grassroots lobbying. Finally, as a consequence of cultural differences in lobbying, the LDA does not sufficiently consider lobbying in national or international associations, which is highly important for interest representation in the EU.

4.4 Incentives for further research

Even if the US lobby register might still be considered as a model for the EU, further research needs to evaluate to what extent the diverging European culture of lobbying would justify sanctions similar to those linked to the LDA. Due to the fact that a major part of the available literature is either written from a scientific perspective or based on personal lobbying experience of one single actor, it is essential that further research concentrates more intensively on broader actors' perception—only this can create a basis for scientific analysis that is sound and realistic.

Since an amended IIA and an improved TR should account for the needs of the register's target group and the extent to which the latter applies the TR, current and representative figures and information should be collected, such as numbers on monthly unique website visitors. Therefore, further research should assess to what extent the TR is applied by MEPs, their personnel, and further staff of EU institutions on a daily basis, and specify how awareness-raising measures could be improved. Further central research questions could be to what extent the general target group regards the register as an essential and time-saving tool; accordingly, which information provided is the most helpful and whether such a register can indeed be applied as a means to increase transparency or improve the public reputation of lobbyists. Equally, these questions could also be the basis for research concentrating on mandatory registration. The EU's semiannual 'Eurobarometer' might be an option to generate at least a part of possible results related to the TR.

Generally, all aspects of improvement discussed in this book during the TR revision procedure essentially require being checked for feasibility before being implemented. Furthermore, additional research should assess whether the findings of the legal study by Krajewski are realistic, and consider the option to harmonize Member States' regulation of political corruption and lobby regulation. Obviously, the implementation of an exceptional formula, which would allow professional consultancies, law firms, and self-employed consultants to justify the disclosure of their clients' names, is rather rejected. Without a doubt, such a formula would also lead to an unequal treatment of registrants. Nonetheless, it might be the only opportunity to actually make more entities of this category to appear in the TR, because with a voluntary approach, the only alternative seems that members of this category voluntarily change their contractual terms. Consequently, potential effects of such a formula should be examined through further research.

Lobbying is an essential element of political decision-making; where the expertise of politicians is limited, it complements legislative preparation where expert knowledge is needed and guarantees that interests of the industry, science, societal groups, and further organizations are appropriately represented vis-à-vis decision makers. As a consequence of the degree of influence that the lobbyists and interest groups gained during the last years, lobby registers are an informative tool for policy makers, and a helpful but also necessary opportunity for the public to gain an overview and background information about those representing interests on their behalf. Irrespective of the fact that even a mandatory register is no guarantee that all relevant actors are covered, a lobbyist is not necessarily good if being a registrant, nor bad if refusing to disclose information. The success of lobbying transparency also highly depends on the consequent willingness of political decision makers to avoid meeting those lobbyists who obviously refuse registration or break the code of conduct. A comprehensive European debate about lobbying regulation at the EU level should be further complemented by the involvement of European public and media. As research has disclosed, the profession of lobbying is not as opaque, secretive, and 'bad' as often perceived. Still, it cannot be fully uncovered through registration.

5 References

AHRENS, K. (¹2007). Nutzen und Grenzen der Regulierung von Lobbying. In: R. Kleinfeld et al. (eds.), *Lobbying. Strukturen. Akteure. Strategien,* Wiesbaden: VS Verlag für Sozialwissenschaften, pp. 124, 125, 140, 142f.

AINSWORTH, S. (¹2010). Methodological Perspectives on Interest Groups. In: L.S. Maisel and J.M. Berry (eds.), *The Oxford Handbook of American Political Parties and Interest Groups.* New York: Oxford University Press Inc., pp. 89, 92.

ALTER-EU. (2012). Dodgy Data. Time to fix the EU's Transparency Register. http://www.alter-eu.org/sites/default/files/documents/Dodgy-data.pdf, visited on May19, 2013, p. 4.

ALTER-EU. (2013). Rescue the Register! How to make EU Lobby Transparency Credible and Reliable. http://www.alter-eu.org/sites/default/files/documents/Rescue_the_Register_report_25June2013.pdf, visited on July 29, 2013, pp. 3, 8, 9, 11, 12.f, 19, 24, 25.

ALTER-EU. (n.d.). About ALTER-EU. http://www.alter-eu.org/about, visited on July 10, 2013.

Arte+7. (n.d.). The Brussels Business. http://www.youtube.com/watch?v=60xbEoDQ4RM, visited on March 2, 13.

BDI EMPLOYEE. (2013). Interview of June 19, 2013.

BERRY, J.M. (³1997). *The Interest Group Society.* NL: Longman, pp. 4, 6f, 8, 19, 24, 31, 96, 108, 116, 173.

BM CONSULTANT. (2013). Interview of July 3, 2013.

BOUWEN, P. (¹2005). Zugangslogik in der Europäischen Union: Der Fall des Europäischen Parlaments. In: R. Eising and B. Kohler-Koch (eds.), *Interessenpolitik in Europa. Regieren in Europa 7.* Baden-Baden: Nomos, p. 98.

BOUWEN, P. (2011). The European Commission. In: D. Coen and J. Richardson (eds.), *Lobbying the European Union: Institutions, Actors, and Issues.* Oxford: Oxford University Press, p. 26.

BROCKHAUS, der. (2008). *Politik. Ideen, Systeme und Prozesse.* Mannheim: F.A. Brockhaus, p. 273.

BUHOLZER, R.P. (1998). *Legislatives Lobbying in der Europäischen Union. Ein Konzept für Interessengruppen.* Dissertation Nr. 2153; Universität Sankt Gallen. Bern: Verlag Paul Haupt, pp. 11, 25, 129, 154, 204, 223, 226.

BURSON-MARSTELLER. (2013). A Guide to Effective Lobbying in Europe. The View of Policy-Makers. http://lobbyingsurvey.burson-marsteller.eu/wp-content/uploads/2013/05/european_lobbying_survey_2013.pdf, visited on June 23, 2013, pp. 16, 18, 22, 23, 67.

BUSINESSEUROPE. (2013). Mission and Priorities. http://www.businesseurope.eu/content/default.asp?PageID=582, visited on July 6, 2013.

BUSINESSEUROPE Employee. (2013). Interview of July 3, 2013.

CENTER FOR RESPONSIVE POLITICS. (2013). Lobbying Database. http://www.open secrets.org/lobby/, visited on May 26, 2013.

CHR EMPLOYEE. (2013). Interview of July 3, 2013.

CINI, M. (^{3}2010). Intergovernmentalism. In: M. Cini and N. Pérez-Solórzano Borragán (eds.), *European Union Politics*. New York: Oxford University Press, pp. 87.

CLEAN UP WASHINGTON. (2005). History of the Lobbying Disclosure Act. http://www.clean upwashington.org/lobbying/page.cfm?pageid=38#_edn1, visited on April 13, 2013.

COEN, D. and RICHARDSON, J. (2011). *Lobbying the European Union: Institutions, Actors, and Issues*. Oxford: Oxford University Press, pp. 11, 21.

COMMISSION OF THE EUROPEAN COMMUNITIES. (2002). Communication from the Commission. Towards a reinforced culture of consultation and dialogue—General principles and minimum standards for consultation of interested parties by the Commission. http://eur-lex.europa.eu/LexUriServ/LexUriServ.do?uri=COM:2002:0704:FIN:EN:PDF, visited on July 15, 2013, p. 4.

COMMISSION REPRESENTATIVE. (2013a). Interview of May 2, 2013.

COMMISSION REPRESENTATIVE. (2013b). E-mail received on May 6, 2013.

COMMISSION REPRESENTATIVE. (2013c). E-mail received on May 7, 2013.

COMMISSION REPRESENTATIVE. (2013d). Comment Made During Live Debate "Mandatory or Voluntary? Time for a Register that Really Works!", European Parliament. June 17, 2013.

CONSILIUM (n.d.). Council Configurations. *http://www.consilium.europa.eu/council/council-configurations?lang=en*, visited on July 13, 2013.

COUNCIL OF THE EUROPEAN UNION. (2008). I Item Note, 11374/08. Approval of a reply to the letter of Mr Hans-Gert PÖTTERING, President of the European Parliament. http://register.consilium.europa.eu/pdf/en/08/st11/st11374.en08.pdf, visited on May 18, 2013.

CRP REPRESENTATIVE. (2013a). E-mail received on June 3, 2013.

CRP REPRESENTATIVE. (2013b). E-mail received on June 21, 2013.

DE CLERCK, P. (2013). Comment raised during live debate "Mandatory or Voluntary? Time for a Register that Really Works!", European Parliament. June 17, 2013.

DeLACY, C. and IRVING, J.S. IV. (2013). U.S. Attorney Seeks $33 Million Lobbying Disclosure Act Penalty. Complaint Signals a More Aggressive Enforcement Policy. http://www.hklaw.com/publications/US-Attorney-Seeks-33-Million-Lobbying-Disclosure-Act-Penalty-06-13-2013/, visited on August 4, 2013.

DLR EMPLOYEE. (2013). Interview of May 27, 2013.

EISING, R. and KOHLER-KOCH, B. (¹2005). Interessenpolitik im europäischen Mehrebenensystem. In: R. Eising and B. Kohler-Koch (eds.), *Interessenpolitik in Europa. Regieren in Europa 7*. Baden-Baden: Nomos, pp. 11, 16, 23, 24, 29.

EISING, R. and LEHRINGER, S. (³2010). Interest Groups and the European Union. In: M. Cini and N. Pérez-Solórzano Borragán (eds.), *European Union Politics*. New York: Oxford University Press, pp. 190, 191, 192, 193, 194, 195, 198, 199, 200, 202, 203, 446.

EU LOBBYING EXPERT. (2013). E-mail received on June 22, 2013.

EU OBSERVER. (2013). EU Losing Again in Lobbying Game. http://euobserver.com/opinion/119528, visited on April 27, 2013.

EUROBOTICS EMPLOYEE. (2013). Interview of June 19, 2013.

EUROPA. (2011a). Q's & A's: Transparency Register. http://europa.eu/rapid/press-release_MEMO-11-446_en.htm?locale=en, visited on May 1, 2013.

EUROPA. (2011b). Parliament Magazine, "Open for Business." http://ec.europa.eu/commission_2010-2014/sefcovic/documents/022-025_parliament_2 7_june.pdf, visited on May 5, 2013, pp. 22, 25.

EUROPA. (2011c). Commission and European Parliament launch Joint Transparency Register to shed light on all those seeking to influence European policy, Press Release. http://europa.eu/rapid/press-release_IP-11-773_en.htm?locale=en, visited on July 19, 2013.

EUROPA. (2012). First Annual Report on Transparency Register shows good start, and sets further objectives for 2013. http://europa.eu/rapid/press-release_IP-12-1265_en.htm, visited on July 12, 2013.

EUROPA. (n.d.a). Glossary: Green Paper. http://europa.eu/legislation_summaries/glossary/green_paper_en.htm, visited on May 5, 2013.

EUROPA. (n.d.b). Glossary: White Paper. http://europa.eu/legislation_summaries/glossary/white_paper_en.htm, visited on May 5, 2013.

EUROPA. (n.d.c). Glossary: Right of Initiative. http://europa.eu/legislation_summaries/glossary/initiative_right_en.htm, visited on July 13, 2013.

EUROPA. (n.d.d). Glossary: Council of the European Union. http://europa.eu/legislation_summaries/glossary/eu_council_en.htm, visited on July 15, 2013.

EUROPA. (n.d.e). Glossary: European Commission. http://europa.eu/legislation_summaries/glossary/european_commission_en.htm, visited on July 15, 2013.

EUROPA. (n.d.f). Register of Commission Expert Groups and Other Similar Entities. Expert Groups explained. http://ec.europa.eu/transparency/regexpert/index.cfm?do=faq.faq&aide=2, visited on June 1, 2013.

EUROPEDIRECT. (2013). E-mail received on August 1, 2013.

EUROPEAN PARLIAMENT. (2006). A 'Rapporteur'—the Person who Presents Reports to Parliament. http://www.europarl.europa.eu/sides/getDoc.do?type=IM-PRESS&reference=20060725STO09938&language=EN, visited April 17, 2013.

EUROPEAN PARLIAMENT. (2008). European Parliament Resolution of May 8, 2008 on the Development of the Framework for the Activities of Interest Representatives (lobbyists) in the European Institutions (2007/2115(INI)). http://www.europarl.europa.eu/sides/getDoc.do?pubRef=-//EP//TEXT+TA+P6-TA-2008-0197+0+DOC+XML+V0//EN, visited on June 12, 2013, 16.

EUROPEAN PARLIAMENT. (2010). The European Parliament. Luxembourg: Publications Office of the European Union, pp. 4, 9.

EUROPEAN PARLIAMENT. (2011). Interinstitutional Agreement on a Common Transparency Register between the Parliament and the Commission. European Parliament Decision of May 11, 2011 on Conclusion of an Interinstitutional Agreement between the European Parliament and the Commission on a Common Transparency Register. http://www.europarl.europa.eu/pdf/lobbyists/2011/P7_TA-PROV(2011)0222_EN.pdf, visited on June 15, 2013, VI 24, Annex IV.

EUROPEAN PARLIAMENT. (2013a). Rules of Procedure. http://www.europarl.europa.eu/sides/getDoc.do?pubRef=-//EP//NONSGML+RULES-EP+20130204+0+DOC+PDF+V0//EN&language=EN, visited on May 1, 2013, pp. 175, 176f.

EUROPEAN PARLIAMENT. (n.d.). Parliamentary Committees. http://www.europarl.europa.eu/aboutparliament/en/00aab6aedf/Committees.html, visited on July 13, 2013.

EUROPEAN UNION. (n.d.). Parliamentary Committees. http://europa.eu/legislation_summaries/glossary/parliamentary_committees_en.htm, visited on April 17, 2013.

EUROSTAT. (2013). Kroatien in der EU in Zahlen. Eurostat Press Release of June 25, 2013. http://epp.eurostat.ec.europa.eu/cache/ITY_PUBLIC/1-25062013-AP/DE/1-2506 2013-AP-DE.PDF, visited on July 12, 2013.

EU WATCHDOG REPRESENTATIVE. (2013a). Interview of April 25, 2013.

EU WATCHDOG REPRESENTATIVE. (2013b). E-mail received on May 6, 2013.

EU WATCHDOG REPRESENTATIVE. (2013c). E-mail received on May 21, 2013.

FRIEDRICH, S. (2010). Measuring Interest Group Activity. CESifo DICE Report 4/2010. http://www.cesifo-group.de/ifoHome/publications/docbase/details.html?docId=14994986, visited on April 21, 2013, pp. 38, 45.

GELLNER, W. and KLEIBER, M. (¹2007). *Das Regierungssystem der USA. Eine Einführung*. Baden-Baden: Nomos Verlagsgesellschaft, pp. 32, 42, 43f, 47, 48, 59, 165.

GENTILI, A. (2013). Transparency Register, Work in Progress. Evaluation of the Register's Effectiveness Before its Second Anniversary and its Review. Evaluation Report. http://www.europeanpublicaffairs.eu/wp-content/uploads/2013/06/Transparency-Register_Evaluation-report_Andrea-Gentili.pdf, visited on June 11, 2013, pp. IV, V, 1, 5, 6, 9, 10, 14.

GREENWOOD, J. and DREGER, J. (2013). The Transparency Register: A European Vanguard of Strong Lobby Regulation? http://www.palgrave-journals.com/iga/journal/v2/n2/full/iga20133a.html, visited on August 9, 2013.

GROSSMANN, M. (2012). *The Not-So-Special Interests. Interest Groups, Public Representation, and American Governance.* Stanford, CA: Stanford University Press, p. 11.

GSC REPRESENTATIVE. (2013). E-mail received on May 15, 2013.

HAAS, C.M. et al. (^{3}2007). Der Kongreß. In: W. Jäger et al. (eds.), *Regierungssystem der USA. Lehr- und Handbuch.* München: Oldenbourg Wissenschaftsverlag GmbH, pp.102, 187.

HANDELSBLATT. (2013). Die 500 größten Unternehmen Europas. No. 110, 12.06.2013, Seite 1, 4–7.

HART, T. (2011). Mehr Transparenz für die stillen Mächtigen. In: Leif et al. and SPETH, R. (eds.), (12003). Die stille Macht. Lobbyismus in Deutschland. Wiesbaden: Westdeutscher Verlag, p. 63Transparency

HIX, S. and HØYLAND, B. (^{3}2011). *The Political System of the European Union.* The European Union Series. Houndmills/New York: Palgrave Macmillan, pp.12, 15, 34, 37, 38, 54, 159, 165, 173, 181.

HOLMAN, C. (2008). Making the U.S. Lobbying Disclosure Act Work as Intended: Implications for the European Transparency Initiative. http://www.citizen.org/documents/Making-LDA-Work.pdf, visited on May 18, 2013, pp. 2, 3, 4, 8, 10, 13, 17.

HOLMAN, C. (2009). Lobbying Reform in the United States and the European Union: Progress on Two Continents. In: C. McGrath (ed.), *Interest Groups and Lobbying in the United States, and Comparative Perspectives.* Lewiston, ME: Edwin Mellen Press. http://www.centreurope-montreal.ca/fileadmin/confluence/2949195/paper_cholman_20 090525.pdf, visited on May 22, 2013.

HOLMAN, C. and LUNEBURG, W. (2012). Lobbying and Transparency: A Comparative Analysis of Regulatory Reform. http://www.palgrave-journals.com/iga/journal/v1/n1/full/iga20124a.html, visited on April 28, 2013.

HOUSE OF REPRESENTATIVES. (1995). Lobbying Disclosure Act of 1995. Report. http://lobbyingdisclosure.house.gov/HReport104-339.pdf, visited on April 23, 2013, p. 6.

HULA, K.W. (1999). *Lobbying Together. Interest Group Coalitions in Legislative Politics.* Washington, DC: Georgetown University Press, pp. 2, 5, 7.

IN-HOUSE LOBBYIST. (2013). Interview of June 14, 2013.

JÄGER, W. et al. (^{3}2007). *Regierungssystem der USA. Lehr- und Handbuch.* München: Oldenbourg Wissenschaftsverlag GmbH, pp. 36f.

JOINT TRANSPARENCY REGISTER SECRETARIAT (JTRS). (2012a). Transparency Register Compliance Guidelines, Edition No. 3. http://ec.europa.eu/transparency register/info/your-organisation/guidanceFinancial.do?locale=en, visited on January 17, 2014, pp. 3f.

JTRS. (2012b). Annual Report on the Operations of the Transparency Register. http://ec.europa.eu/transparencyregister/info/about-register/reportsAndPublications.do? locale=en, visited on January 15, 2014, Chapters 1.1, 1.2.1, 1.3.2.1, 1.3.2.2, 1.3.2.3, 2.2, 2.3, 3.1.2, 3.2, 3.3., 3.3.2, pp. 4, 5, 13, 14, 15.

JTRS. (2012c). Transparency Register. Frequently Asked Questions. http://ec.europa.eu/transparencyregister/info/your-organisation/faq.do?locale=en, visited on January 16, 2014, p. 3.

JTRS. (2013). Transparency Register Statistics. http://ec.europa.eu/transparency/docs/reg/new_statistiques_en.pdf, visited on July 29, 2013.

JOURNALS OF THE RESEARCH GROUP ON SOCIALISM AND DEMOCRACY ONLINE. (2012). Lobbying in the European Commission: Open or Secret? http://sdonline.org/56/volume-25-no-2/lobbying-the-european-commission-open-or-secret1/, visited on March 29, 2013.

JTRS STAFF. (2013a). Interview of May 15, 2013.

JTRS STAFF. (2013b). E-mail received on May 21, 2013.

JTRS STAFF. (2013c). E-mail received on May 27, 2013.

JTRS STAFF. (2013d). E-mail received on June 4, 2013.

KLÜVER, H. (2012). Interessenvermittlung in der Europäischen Union. Nationale Verbände auf dem Weg nach Brüssel. Saarbrücken: AV Akademiker Verlag, p. 22, 52.

KOLLMAN, K. (1998). *Outside Lobbying. Public Opinion & Interest Group Strategies.* Princeton, NJ: Princeton University Press, p. Xiii.

KRAFT, E. (2006). *Lobbying in der EU. Regulierung nach US-Vorbild?* Saarbrücken: VDM Verlag Dr. Müller, pp. 9, 18f, 27, 28, 29, 35, 39, 48, 49, 50.

KRAJEWSKI, M. (2013a). *Legal Study. Legal Framework for a Mandatory EU Lobby Register and Regulations.* Erlangen-Nürnberg: University of Erlangen-Nürnberg, p. 3, 4, 6, 7, 9, 10.

KRAJEWSKI, M. (2013b). Comment raised during live debate "Mandatory or Voluntary? Time for a Register That Really Works!", European Parliament. June 17, 2013.

LAHUSEN, C. (^{1}2005). Kommerzielle Beratungsfirmen in der Europäischen Union. In: R. Eising and B. Kohler-Koch (eds.), *Interessenpolitik in Europa. Regieren in Europa 7.* Baden-Baden: Nomos, p. 251.

LEIF, T. and SPETH, R. (eds.), (^{1}2003). *Die stille Macht. Lobbyismus in Deutschland.* Wiesbaden: Westdeutscher Verlag, p. 8, 28.

LEVIN, R.M. (2011). Lobbying Law in the Spotlight: 'Challenges and Proposed Improvements Report of the Task Force on Federal Lobbying Laws'. Section of Administrative Law and Regulatory Practice American Bar Association. http://www.americanbar.org/content/dam/aba/migrated/2011_build/administrative_law/lobbying_task_force_report_010311.authcheckdam.pdf, visited on May 13, 2013, pp. vii, 5.

LOBBYING DISCLOSURE ACT OF 1995. (2007). http://www.senate.gov/legislative/ Lobbying/Lobby_Disclosure_Act/compilation.pdf, visited on May 19, 2013, s. 2(1)(2)(3); s. 3 (13), (14); s. 4(a)(2)(3), (b)(1)(2)(3)(5)(6), (c); s. 5(b)(4)(5); 5(c)(1)(2); 5(d)(1)(A)(B)(C)(D); s. 6(a)(1)(2)(4)(8)(11),(5), (b)(2); s. 7(1),(2); s. 8 (a)(1)(2)(3), (c); s. 26 (a),(b)(1).

LOBBYPEDIA. (2013). Lobbyregister (Überblick). https://lobbypedia.de/wiki/Lobbyregister_%28%C3%9Cberblick%29#D.C3.A4nemark, visited on August 9, 2013.

MACOVEI, M. (MEP). (2013). Represented through her assistant during live debate "Mandatory or Voluntary? Time for a Register That Really Works!" European Parliament. June 17, 2013.

MAGLOFF, L. (2013). Federal Lobbying Guidelines. http://smallbusiness.chron.com/federal-lobbying-guidelines-14110.html, visited on March 31, 2013.

McFARLAND, A. (^{1}2010). Interest Group Theory. In: L. Maisel et al. *The Oxford Handbook of American Political Parties and Interest Groups.* New York: Oxford University Press Inc., p. 50.

MEP. (2013). Interview of May 29, 2013.

MICHALOWITZ, I. (2007). *Lobbying in der EU.* Wien: facultas wuv, pp. 51, 52, 71, 73, 78, 79, 88, 90, 172, 174, 177, 179, 181, 183.

MOSER, C. (2001). *How Open is 'Open as Possible'? Three Different Approaches to Transparency and Openness in Regulating Access to EU Documents.* Vienna: Institute for Advanced Studies, Political Science Series, No. 80, pp. 2, 3, 4, 5.

NAURIN, D. (2004). *Dressed for Politics. Why Increasing Transparency in the European Union Will Not Make Lobbyists Behave Any Better Than They Already Do.* Göteborg: Department of Political Science Göteborg, pp. 12.

NUGENT, N. (^{7}2010). *The Government and Politics of the European Union. The European Union Series.* Houndmills (UK)/New York: Palgrave MacMillan, pp. 105, 183, 245, 249, 250, 251, 252.

OBRADOVIC, D. (2011). Regulating Lobbying in the European Union. In: D. Coen and J. Richardson (eds.), *Lobbying the European Union: Institutions, Actors, and Issues.* Oxford: Oxford University Press, p. 318.

OECD. (2010a). Recommendation of the Council on Principles for Transparency and Integrity in Lobbying. http://acts.oecd.org/Instruments/ShowInstrumentView.aspx?InstrumentID=256&InstrumentPID=%20250, visited on July 7, 2013.

OECD. (2010b). Transparency and Integrity in Lobbying. http://ec.europa.eu/enlargement/taiex/dyn/create_speech.jsp?speechID=16281&key=c39c5ed4225bb66e3049c5ad72f54783, visited on January 16, 2013.

OFFICE OF THE CLERK. (2013a). Lobbying Disclosure Act Guidance. http://lobbyingdisclosure.house.gov/amended_lda_guide.html, visited on March 29, 2013, s. 2, 3, 4, 5, 6, 7, 8.

OFFICE OF THE CLERK. (2013b). Notifications and Announcements. http://lobbying disclosure.house.gov/, visited on April 13, 2013.

OFFICE OF THE CLERK. 113th Congress. 1st Session. Public Disclosure. http://clerk.house.gov/public_disc/index.aspx, visited on August 5, 2013.

OFFICIAL OF THE COUNCIL. (2013a). Interview of April 26, 2013.

OFFICIAL OF THE COUNCIL. (2013b). E-mail received on July 9, 2013.

OFFICIAL JOURNAL OF THE EUROPEAN UNION. (2009). 2009/C 271 E/06. 11, 16, p. 50.

OFFICIAL JOURNAL OF THE EUROPEAN UNION. (2011). Interinstitutional Agreement. Agreement between the European Parliament and the European Commission on the Establishment of a Transparency Register for Organisations and Self-employed Individuals Engaged in EU Policy-making and Policy implementation. http://eur-lex.europa.eu/LexUriServ/LexUriServ.do?uri=OJ:L:2011:191:0029:0038:EN:PDF, visited on May 1, 2013, I. (4), IV. (8), VIII., VIII. (28.), Arts 21 and 22, Annexes I and II.

PATRICK, J.J. et al. ([5]2002). *The Oxford Guide to the United States Government.* Oxford: Oxford University Press, hearings, congressional.

PLATZER, H.-W. (2008). Interessenverbände und europäischer Lobbyismus. In: W. Weidenfeld (ed.), *Die Europäische Union. Politisches System und Politikbereiche.* Bonn: Bundeszentrale für politische Bildung, pp. 187, 200.

PLATZER, H.-W. (2010). *Europäische Arbeitgeber- und Wirtschaftsverbände.* In: W. Schroeder and B. Weßels (eds.), Handbuch Arbeitgeber- und Wirtschaftsverbände in Deutschland. Wiesbaden: Verlag für Sozialwissenschaften, p. 435.

PRENZEL, T. (2007). *Handbuch Lobbyarbeit Konkret.* Schwalbach: WOCHENSCHAU Verlag, pp. 10, 12.

RICHARDSON, J. ([3]2006). *European Union. Power and Policy-Making.* Abingdon, Oxon: Routledge, pp. 149, 263.

RITTERSHOFER, C. (2007). Lexikon Politik, Staat, Gesellschaft. 3600 aktuelle Begriffe von Abberufung bis Zwölfmeilenzone. München: dtv, p. 674.

ROSENTHAL, A. (1993). *The Third House. Lobbyists and Lobbying in the States.* Washington, DC: Congressional Quarterly Inc., pp. 22, 122, 150, 189.

SALISBURY, R.H. ([2]1990). The Paradox of Interest Groups in Washington—More Groups, Less Clout. In: A. King et al. (ed.), *The New American Political System.* Lanham, MD: University Press of America Inc., p. 226.

SEBALDT, M. ([1]2007). Strukturen des Lobbying: Deutschland und die USA im Vergleich. In: R. Kleinfeld et al. (eds.), *Lobbying. Strukturen. Akteure. Strategien.* Wiesbaden: VS Verlag für Sozialwissenschaften, pp. 104, 105.

SEBALDT, M. (2011). Transformation der Verbändedemokratie. Die Modernisierung des Systems organisierter Interessen in den USA. Wiesbaden: Westdeutscher Verlag GmbH, pp. 69, 95, 102.

ŠEFČOVIČ, M. (2011). Lobbyismus braucht Transparenz. Das neue Transparenz-Register des Europäischen Parlaments und der Europäischen Kommission. In: Recht und Politik, Ausgabe 04/2011, Berlin: Berliner Wirtschaftsverlag. http://ec.europa.eu/commis sion_2010-2014/sefcovic/headlines/articles/2011/12/index_en.htm, visited on May 21, 2013, pp.198f, 200, 201, 202.

ŠEFČOVIČ, M. (2013). Speech—Opening Remarks. OECD Forum on Transparency and Integrity in Lobbying of June 27, 2013. http://europa.eu/rapid/press-release_SPEECH-13-581_en.htm?locale=en, visited on July 29, 2013.

SENIOR CONSULTANT OF A NONREGISTERED BRUSSELS-BASED CONSULTANCY. (2012). Telephone interview of June 12, 2013.

STRAUS, J.R. (2008). Honest Leadership and Open Government Act of 2007: The Role of the Clerk of the House and Secretary of the Senate. http://www.fas.org/sgp/crs/ secrecy/RL34377.pdf, visited on August 2, 2013.

STRAUS, J.R. (2011). Lobbying Registration and Disclosure: Before and After the Enactment of the Honest Leadership and Open Government Act of 2007. http://www.fas.org/sgp/crs/misc/R40245.pdf, visited on April 12, 2013, pp. 1, 8.

STRAUS, J.R. (2013). Lobbying Registration and Disclosure: The Role of the Clerk of the House and the Secretary of the Senate. http://www.fas.org/sgp/crs/misc/RL34377.pdf, visited on April 13, 2013, pp. summary, 2, 5.

THUNERT, M. ([1]2003). Is that the way we like it? Lobbying in den USA. In: T. Leif and R. Speth (eds.), *Die stille Macht. Lobbyismus in Deutschland.* Wiesbaden: Westdeutscher Verlag, pp. 321f, 325, 331.

TRANSPARENCY REGISTER. (2013a). Who is Expected to Register? http://ec.europa.eu/ transparencyregister/info/your-organisation/whoRegister.do?locale=en, visited on January 17, 2014.

TRANSPARENCY REGISTER. (2013b). Shell Companies. http://ec.europa.eu/transpa rencyregister/public/consultation/displaylobbyist.do?id=05032108616-26, visited on August 10, 2013.

TRANSPARENCY REGISTER. (2013c). Search Register. http://ec.europa.eu/transpa rencyregister/public/consultation/search.do?locale=en&reset=, visited on August 13, 2013.

UNITED STATES CENSUS BUREAU. (2013). U.S. and World Population Clock. http://www.census.gov/popclock/, visited on August 5, 2013.

US GOVERNMENT ACCOUNTABILITY OFFICE (GAO). (2013). 2012 Lobbying Disclosure. Observations on Lobbyists' Compliance with Disclosure Requirements. http://www.gao.gov/assets/660/653471.pdf, visited on August 4, 2013, pp. highlights page, 12, 13, 16, 18, 20, 22.

UNITED STATES HOUSE OF REPRESENTATIVES. (n.d.). The Legislative Process; In Committee; House Floor; To the Senate. http://www.house.gov/content/learn/legislative _process/, visited on July 20, 2013.

UNITED STATES SENATE. (n.d.a). Query the Lobbying Disclosure Act Database. http://soprweb.senate.gov/index.cfm?event=processSearchCriteria, visited on August 10, 2013.

UNITED STATES SENATE. (n.d.b). Query the Lobbying Contributions Database. http://soprweb.senate.gov/index.cfm?event=lobbyistSelectFields&reset=1, visited on August 10, 2013.

US CONGRESS, HOUSE COMMITTEE ON THE JUDICIARY. (1995). *Lobbying Disclosure Act of 1995, report to accompany H.R. 2564*, 104th Cong., 1st sess., H.Rept. 104-339. Washington: GPO, p. 2.

USINFO. (n.d.). The President of the United States: Legislative Powers. http://usinfo.org/enus/government/branches/ben_president2.html, visited on July 20, 2013.

US WATCHDOG REPRESENTATIVE. (2013a). E-mail received on May 21, 2013.

US WATCHDOG REPRESENTATIVE. (2013b). E-mail received on May 26, 2013.

VAN SCHENDELEN, R. (1993). *National Public and Private EC Lobbying*. Aldershot: Dartmouth, p. 14.

VAN SCHENDELEN, R. ([1]2012). *Die Kunst des EU-Lobbyings. Erfolgreiches Public Affairs Management im Labyrinth Brüssels*. Berlin: Lexxion Verlagsgesellschaft mbH Berlin, pp. VII, 61, 62, 63, 81, 82, 83, 84, 148, 188f, 385.

WALLACE, H. et al. ([6]2010). *Policy-Making in the European Union*. The New European Union Series. Oxford: Oxford University Press, pp. 391, 392.

WASSER, H. ([3]2007). Interessengruppen. In: Jäger, W. et al. (eds.), *Regierungssystem der USA. Lehr- und Handbuch*. München: Oldenbourg Wissenschaftsverlag GmbH, pp. 336, 339.

WEIDENFELD, W. and WESSEL, W. (eds.). (2011). *Europa von A bis Z*. Schriftenreihe, Band 1123. Bundeszentrale für pol. Bonn: Bildung, pp. 360, 361, 363.

WILSON, J.Q. et al. ([12]2011). *American Government. Institutions and Policies*. Boston: Cengage Learning, pp. 8, 31, 52, 261–264, 272f, 277, 281, 314, 336, 341, 342, 349.

WOLL, C. (2006). Research agenda. Lobbying in the European Union: From sui generis to a comparative perspective. *Journal of European Public Policy*, **13** (3), pp. 1-14

WWF EMPLOYEE. (2013). Interview of May 28, 2013.

6 Annex

6.1 Databases

(I) TR search result for Shell Companies[618]

Profile of registrant	
Shell Companies	
Identification number in the register: **05032108616-26**	
Registration date: **18/04/12 10:36:21**	
The information on this organisation was last modified on **15/04/13 12:52:31**	
The date of the last annual update was **15/04/13 12:52:31**	

Registrant : Organisation or self-employed individual	
Name/company name:	**Shell Companies**
Acronym:	**Shell**
Legal status:	**Royal Dutch Shell plc directly or indirectly holds shares in Shell Companies. Royal Dutch Shell plc is a public Limited Company with its registered offices in the United Kingdom and headquartered in The Hague, the Netherlands.**
Website address:	http://www.shell.com

Sections	
Section:	**II - In-house lobbyists and trade/professional associations**
and more precisely:	**Companies & groups**

Person with legal responsibility	
Surname, Name:	**Mr Peter Voser**
Position:	**Chief Executive Officer**

Permanent person in charge of EU relations	
Surname, Name:	**Mr Ivan Martin**
Position:	**Head of European Union Liaison for Shell Companies**

Contact details:	
Contact details of organisation's head office:	**30 Carel van Bylandtlaan** **The Hague 2596 HR** **NETHERLANDS**
Telephone number:	**(+31) 703771000**
Fax number:	**(+)**
Other contact information:	

---

[618] Transparency Register. (2013b) "Shell Companies". http://ec.europa.eu/transparency register/public/consultation/displaylobbyist.do?id=05032108616-26, visited on August 10, 2013.

(II) Search engine TR[619]

Find registrants	
with register identification number:	
with name / company name:	
with acronym:	
whose legally responsible person is:	
whose permanent person in charge of EU relations is:	
whose accredited person for access to the European Parliament is:	
with head office in:	
with registration date since:	

(III) SOS LDA database for LD-2 reports[620]

Registrant Name	Client Name	Filing Type	Amount Reported	Date Posted	Filing Year
Cove Strategies	Walmart	FIRST QUARTER REPORT	$50,000.00	04/22/2013	2013
Cove Strategies	Walmart	SECOND QUARTER REPORT	$60,000.00	07/19/2013	2013
Cove Strategies	Walmart	FOURTH QUARTER REPORT	$40,000.00	01/22/2013	2012
Cove Strategies	Walmart	FIRST QUARTER REPORT	$40,000.00	04/19/2012	2012
Cove Strategies	Walmart	SECOND QUARTER REPORT	$40,000.00	07/20/2012	2012
Cove Strategies	Walmart	THIRD QUARTER REPORT	$40,000.00	10/22/2012	2012
Cove Strategies	Walmart	FOURTH QUARTER REPORT	$40,000.00	01/19/2012	2011
Cove Strategies	Walmart	REGISTRATION		09/15/2011	2011
Cove Strategies	Walmart	THIRD QUARTER REPORT	$40,000.00	10/19/2011	2011
Registrant Name	Client Name	Filing Type	Amount Reported	Date Posted	Filing Year

Showing 1 to 9 of 9 entries

---

[619] Transparency Register. (2013c). Search Register. http://ec.europa.eu/transparencyregister/public/consultation/search.do?locale=en&reset=, visited on August 13, 2013.

[620] United States Senate. (n.d.a). Query the Lobbying Disclosure Act Database. http://soprweb.senate.gov/index.cfm?event=processSearchCriteria, visited on August 10, 2013.

(IV) SOS database for reports about certain contributions (LD-203)[621]

Registrant Name	Lobbyist Name	Filing Type	Filing Year	Date Posted
VOLKSWAGEN GROUP OF AMERICA INC	SCHNEIDER, ANNA-MARIA	LD-203 MID-YEAR REPORT	2013	07/29/2013
VOLKSWAGEN GROUP OF AMERICA INC		LD-203 MID-YEAR REPORT	2013	07/30/2013
VOLKSWAGEN GROUP OF AMERICA INC	SCHNEIDER, ANNA-MARIA	LD-203 MID-YEAR REPORT	2012	07/30/2012
VOLKSWAGEN GROUP OF AMERICA INC		LD-203 MID-YEAR REPORT	2012	07/30/2012
VOLKSWAGEN GROUP OF AMERICA INC	SCHNEIDER, ANNA-MARIA	LD-203 YEAR-END REPORT	2012	01/30/2013
VOLKSWAGEN GROUP OF AMERICA INC		LD-203 YEAR-END REPORT	2012	01/30/2013
VOLKSWAGEN GROUP OF AMERICA INC	SCHNEIDER, ANNA-MARIA	LD-203 MID-YEAR REPORT	2011	07/07/2011

6.2 Interview manual

(1) Why did your organization decide for registration with the TR?

(2) Would you regard registration a matter of reputation?/Does the TR evoke a certain kind of peer pressure among interest representatives to join it?

(3) Do you regard the EP access badge or the Commission's e-mail alert mechanism an advantage for lobbyists?/Should the TR be more incentivized?

(4) Do you perceive TR-linked consequences for nonobedience a disadvantage for registered entities?

(5) How much time did the registration procedure take? Did you face any difficulties?

(6) How do you perceive the complexity of registration requirements?/Which requirements should be clarified?

(7) What else would you change about the TR?

(8) Was there any information your organization would have preferred not to disclose?

(9) Would you support the suggestion to check all TR entries immediately after registration?

(10) The JTRS officially relies on the public as well as on watchdogs to monitor the TR. From your perception, is this a good idea or does the JTRS "outsource" its responsibility?/Are random checks sufficient?

---

[621] United States Senate. (n.d.b). Query the Lobbying Contributions Database. http://soprweb.senate.gov/index.cfm?event=lobbyistSelectFields&reset=1, visited on August 10, 2013.

(11) Would you favor the implementation of a mandatory register?/What are the advantages and disadvantages?

(12) Would you favor the idea of being given an access pass for the European Commission as well?

(13) Would you support the suggestion that the Council of Ministers should become the TR's third official operator?

(14) As a consequence to nonobedience of registration rules, in the United States, lobbyists may face civil fines of up to $200,000 or imprisonment of up to five years. Do you regard this as an appropriate punishment for a mandatory register?/What kind of sanctions should be linked to a mandatory register?

(15) To which extent are lobbyists necessary for the political process at all?

6.3 Interviewee overview

Actors'/experts' names	Institutions
BDI Employee, member of the Brussels office of The German Business Representation (BDI), Actor	The German Business Representation, national association
BM Consultant, employee of the Brussels office of the PR and communications firm Burson-Marsteller, Actor	Burson-Marsteller, professional consultancy
BUSINESSEUROPE Employee, associate of BUSINESSEUROPE, Actor	BUSINESS EUROPE, horizontal European business association
CHR Employee, representing the Clerk of the House, House of Representatives, Actor	House of Representatives, US Congress
Commission Representative, Member of the Cabinet of Commission Vice President Maroš Šefčovič, Commissioner for Inter-Institutional Relations and Administration, Actor	EU Commission
CRP Representative, Senior Researcher at the CRP, Expert	CRP, Watchdog Organization
Council Official, Official of the Council's Secretariat, Actor	Council of the EU
DLR Employee, member of the Brussels office of the *German Aerospace Center* (DLR), Actor	German Aerospace Center, Think tanks, research, and academic institutions
EU Lobbying Expert, one of the most important recent scholars on EU lobbying, Expert	European University, Scientist

euRobotics Employee, representative of euRobotics, a newly established European association, Actor	euRobotics, European association
EU Watchdog Representative, former employee of the Brussels-based ALTER-EU, Actor	ALTER-EU, Watchdog organization
GSC Representative, Official working for the GSC of the EU, Actor	Council of the EU
In-House Lobbyist, Head of Brussels office of one of the 10 biggest European companies, Actor	Industrial representative, In-house lobbyists and trade/professional associations
JTRS Staff, Actor	JTRS
MEP, Member and Vice President of the EP, Actor	EP
US Watchdog Representative, Government Affairs Lobbyist working for Public Citizen's Congress Watch, Expert	Public Citizen's Congress Watch, Watchdog organization
WWF Employee, member of the Brussels European Policy Office of the WWF, Actor	WWF, NGOs

AN INTERDISCIPLINARY SERIES
OF THE CENTRE FOR INTERCULTURAL AND EUROPEAN STUDIES

INTERDISZIPLINÄRE SCHRIFTENREIHE
DES CENTRUMS FÜR INTERKULTURELLE UND EUROPÄISCHE STUDIEN

CINTEUS • Fulda University of Applied Sciences • Hochschule Fulda

ISSN 1865-2255

1   Julia Neumeyer
    Malta and the European Union
    A small island state and its way into a powerful community
    ISBN 978-3-89821-814-6

2   Beste İşleyen
    The European Union in the Middle East Peace Process
    A Civilian Power?
    ISBN 978-3-89821-896-2

3   Pia Tamke
    Die Europäisierung des deutschen Apothekenrechts
    Europarechtliche Notwendigkeit und nationalrechtliche Vertretbarkeit einer
    Liberalisierung
    ISBN 978-3-89821-964-8

4   Stamatia Devetzi und Hans-Wolfgang Platzer (Hrsg.)
    Offene Methode der Koordinierung und Europäisches Sozialmodell
    Interdisziplinäre Perspektiven
    ISBN 978-3-89821-994-5

5   Andrea Rudolf
    Biokraftstoffpolitik und Ernährungssicherheit
    Die Auswirkungen der EU-Politik auf die Nahrungsmittelproduktion am
    Beispiel Brasilien
    ISBN 978-3-8382-0099-6

6   Gudrun Hentges / Justyna Staszczak
    Geduldet, nicht erwünscht
    Auswirkungen der Bleiberechtsregelung auf die Lebenssituation geduldeter
    Flüchtlinge in Deutschland
    ISBN 978-3-8382-0080-4

7   Barbara Lewandowska-Tomaszczyk / Hanna Pułaczewska (Eds. / Hrsg.)
    Intercultural Europe
    Arenas of Difference, Communication and Mediation
    ISBN 978-3-8382-0198-6

8   Janina Henning
    In Dubio Pro Europa?
    An Analysis of the European External Action Structures
    after the Treaty of Lisbon
    ISBN 978-3-8382-0298-1

9   Claas Oehlmann
    Europa auf dem Weg zur Recycling-Gesellschaft?
    Die EU-Rohstoffinitiative im Kontext der Strategie Europa 2020
    ISBN 978-3-8382-0401-7

10 Volker Hinnenkamp / Hans-Wolfgang Platzer (Eds. / Hrsg.)
    Interkulturalität und Europäische Integration
    ISBN 978-3-8382-0573-1

11 Vera Axyonova
    The European Union's Democratization Policy for Central Asia
    Failed in Success or Succeeded in Failure?
    ISBN 978-3-8382-0614-1

12 Lisa Moessing
    Lobbying Uncovered?
    Lobbying Registration in the European Union and the United States
    ISBN 978-3-8382-0616-5

Sie haben die Wahl:

Bestellen Sie die
Interdisziplinäre Schriftenreihe des Centrums für interkulturelle und europäische Studien
einzeln oder im **Abonnement**

per E-Mail: vertrieb@ibidem-verlag.de | per Fax (0511/262 2201)
als Brief (*ibidem*-Verlag | Leuschnerstr. 40 | 30457 Hannover)

Bestellformular

☐ Ich abonniere die *Interdisziplinäre Schriftenreihe des Centrums für interkulturelle und europäische Studien* ab Band # _____

☐ Ich bestelle die folgenden Bände der *Interdisziplinären Schriftenreihe des Centrums für interkulturelle und europäische Studien*
____; ____; ____; ____; ____; ____; ____; ____; ____; ____

Lieferanschrift:

Vorname, Name ....

Anschrift ....

E-Mail.. | Tel.: ....

Datum .... | Unterschrift ....

Ihre Abonnement-Vorteile im Überblick:

- Sie erhalten jedes Buch der Schriftenreihe pünktlich zum Erscheinungstermin – immer aktuell, ohne weitere Bestellung durch Sie.
- Das Abonnement ist jederzeit kündbar.
- Die Lieferung ist innerhalb Deutschlands versandkostenfrei.
- Bei Nichtgefallen können Sie jedes Buch innerhalb von 14 Tagen an uns zurücksenden.

***ibidem*-**Verlag
Melchiorstr. 15
D-70439 Stuttgart
info@ibidem-verlag.de

www.ibidem-verlag.de
www.ibidem.eu
www.edition-noema.de
www.autorenbetreuung.de